1st EDITION

Perspectives on Modern World History

The Creation of the State of Israel

1st EDITION

Perspectives on Modern World History

The Creation of the State of Israel

Myra Immell

Book Editor

GREENHAVEN PRESS
A part of Gale, Cengage Learning

GALE
CENGAGE Learning·

Detroit • New York • San Francisco • New Haven, Conn • Waterville, Maine • London

Christine Nasso, *Publisher*
Elizabeth Des Chenes, *Managing Editor*

© 2010 Thomson Gale, a part of Gale, Cengage Learning.

Gale and Greenhaven Press are registered trademarks used herein under license.

For more information, contact:
Greenhaven Press
27500 Drake Rd.
Farmington Hills, MI 48331-3535
Or you can visit our Internet site at gale.cengage.com

For product information and technology assistance, contact us at
Gale Customer Support, 1-800-877-4253.

For permission to use material from this text or product, submit all requests online at
www.cengage.com/permissions.

Further permissions questions can be emailed to permissionrequest@cengage.com

Articles in Greenhaven Press anthologies are often edited for length to meet page requirements. In addition, original titles of these works are changed to clearly present the main thesis and to explicitly indicate the author's opinion. Every effort is made to ensure that Greenhaven Press accurately reflects the original intent of the authors. Every effort has been made to trace the owners of copyrighted material.

Cover images copyright Hiroko Masuike/Getty Images and Bettmann/Corbis. Reproduced by permission.

LIBRARY OF CONGRESS CATALOGING-IN-PUBLICATION DATA

The creation of the state of Israel / Myra Immell, book editor.
    p. cm. -- (Perspectives on modern world history)
    Includes bibliographical references and index.
    ISBN 978-0-7377-4556-6 (hardcover)
1. Israel--History--Declaration of Independence, 1948--Juvenile literature. 2. Palestine--History--1929-1948--Juvenile literature. 3. Israel--History--1948-1967--Juvenile literature. 4. Jews--History--20th century--Juvenile literature. 5. Israel--History--Declaration of Independence, 1948--Sources--Juvenile literature. 6. Palestine--History--1929-1948--Sources--Juvenile literature. 7. Israel--History--1948-1967--Sources--Juvenile literature. 8. Jews--History--20th century--Sources--Juvenile literature. I. Immell, Myra.
    DS126.4.C69 2009
    956.94'04--dc22
                                                            2009024199

Printed in the United States of America
1 2 3 4 5 6 7 13 12 11 10 09

CONTENTS

secure and has the full support of the people. Israel is seen as the most stable regime in the Middle East.

tition nor recognized the state of Israel until borders were officially agreed upon.

CHAPTER 3   ## Personal Narratives

Jerusalem's Hebrew University in 1947 and 1948 tells how she and friends celebrated the outcome of the United Nations' vote to partition Palestine. She describes the emotions evoked by Israeli prime minister David Ben-Gurion's victory speech.

FOREWORD

"History cannot give us a program for the future, but it can give us a fuller understanding of ourselves, and of our common humanity, so that we can better face the future."

—Robert Penn Warren,
American poet and novelist

The history of each nation is punctuated by momentous events that represent turning points for that nation, with an impact felt far beyond its borders. These events—displaying the full range of human capabilities, from violence, greed, and ignorance to heroism, courage, and strength—are nearly always complicated and multifaceted. Any student of history faces the challenge of grasping the many strands that constitute such world-changing events as wars, social movements, and environmental disasters. But understanding these significant historic events can be enhanced by exposure to a variety of perspectives, whether of people involved intimately or of ones observing from a distance of miles or years. Understanding can also be increased by learning about the controversies surrounding such events and exploring hot-button issues from multiple angles. Finally, true understanding of important historic events involves knowledge of the events' human impact—of the ways such events affected people in their everyday lives—all over the world.

Perspectives on Modern World History examines global historic events from the twentieth-century onward by presenting analysis and observation from numerous vantage points. Each volume offers high school, early college level, and general interest readers a thematically arranged anthology of previously published materials that address a major historical event, with an emphasis on international coverage. Each volume opens with background information on the event, then presents the controversies surrounding that event, and concludes with first-person narratives from people who lived through the event or were affected by it. By providing primary sources from the time of the event, as well as relevant commentary surrounding the event, this series can be used to inform debate, help develop critical thinking skills, increase global awareness, and enhance an understanding of international perspectives on history.

Material in each volume is selected from a diverse range of sources, including journals, magazines, newspapers, nonfiction books, personal narratives, speeches, congressional testimony, government documents, pamphlets, organization newsletters, and position papers. Articles taken from these sources are carefully edited and introduced to provide context and background. Each volume of Perspectives on Modern World History includes an array of views on events of global significance. Much of the material comes from international sources and from U.S. sources that provide extensive international coverage.

Each volume in the Perspectives on Modern World History series also includes:

- A full-color **world map**, offering context and geographic perspective.
- An annotated **table of contents** that provides a brief summary of each essay in the volume.
- An **introduction** specific to the volume topic.
- For each viewpoint, a brief **introduction** that has notes about the author and source of the viewpoint, and that provides a summary of its main points.
- Full-color **charts**, **graphs**, **maps**, and other visual representations.

- Informational **sidebars** that explore the lives of key individuals, give background on historical events, or explain scientific or technical concepts.
- A **glossary** that defines key terms, as needed.
- A **chronology** of important dates preceding, during, and immediately following the event.
- A **bibliography** of additional books, periodicals, and Web sites for further research.
- A comprehensive **subject index** that offers access to people, places, and events cited in the text.

Perspectives on Modern World History is designed for a broad spectrum of readers who want to learn more about not only history but also current events, political science, government, international relations, and sociology—students doing research for class assignments or debates, teachers and faculty seeking to supplement course materials, and others wanting to improve their understanding of history. Each volume of Perspectives on Modern World History is designed to illuminate a complicated event, to spark debate, and to show the human perspective behind the world's most significant happenings of recent decades.

INTRODUCTION

Immigration is at the very heart of the state of Israel. *Olim*, Hebrew for those who immigrate to Israel, began arriving long before Israel was proclaimed a state in 1948 and continue to come to the present day. *Olim* built Israel, gave it its unique character and culture, and in the process created an independent state.

Traditional Jewish belief holds that the Land of Israel was given to the Jewish people by God. They have been making *aliyah*, large-scale Jewish immigration to the Land of Israel, since biblical times. In modern times before statehood, during Ottoman rule and the British Mandate of Palestine, there were five numbered *aliyot* (plural of *aliyah*). The first was between 1882 and 1903. It laid the foundation for Jewish settlement in Israel. Between twenty thousand and thirty thousand *olim*—mostly from eastern Europe, some from Yemen—arrived in Palestine. Most came for religious reasons, seeking refuge from the Jewish persecution and pogroms in their own countries. By 1903 they had bought almost ninety thousand acres of land and founded twenty new settlements.

During the Second Aliyah, 1904–1914, forty thousand more eastern European and Yemeni immigrants arrived in Palestine. This influx of immigrants created the first enduring framework for the future establishment of the state of Israel and is considered by many the most important and influential *aliyah* of the five. Several *kibbutzim*, collective farms or settlements, were established and Tel Aviv, the first modern all-Jewish city in Palestine, was founded. Political parties were created and workers' agricultural organizations began to form. Hebrew was revived as a modern, spoken language, and

Hebrew literature and newspapers were published. The first health and welfare organizations were formed, the first bank was founded, the Jewish National Fund (JNF) was established, and the first Jewish self-defense organization in Palestine came into being.

The Third Aliyah, 1919–1923, brought about thirty-five thousand new immigrants, mainly from eastern European countries, almost half from Russia. These *olim* established more new institutions, organizations, and forms of settlement.

In his 1976 work, *Immigration Without Integration: Third World Jews in Israel,* Avraham Shama characterizes the *olim* of the first three *aliyot*:

> The members of the first three aliyot were dedicated individuals. For a person to abandon his home and migrate to a new country requires a readiness to make great adjustments and changes in his life. Migration to Palestine required a commitment beyond that required for migration elsewhere. The Jewish population was small and scattered. The political environment was hostile or at best indifferent to the plight of the Jews. Amenities were almost nonexistent. Living conditions were hard; malaria and other diseases were endemic. The future was uncertain. Admittedly, most Jews who migrated from Europe went to America. Given the harsh conditions in Palestine, this is not surprising. But those who did go to Palestine were committed individuals, convinced that their privations would bear fruit in the form of a livable Jewish state. They were chalutzim (pioneers) and viewed themselves accordingly—as only the first of many to settle in the Land of Israel.

The Fourth Aliyah, 1924–1928, brought yet another eighty-two thousand *olim* to Palestine. While most came from eastern Europe, Poland in particular, smaller numbers came from Asia, the rest of Europe, and America. They began small businesses and workshops in the growing cities, strengthened the towns, promoted industrial development, and restored Jewish labor in the villages.

During the Fifth Aliyah, 1932–1939, more than two hundred thousand new immigrants arrived in Palestine. This group was different. Many were from upper- and middle-class backgrounds and were highly educated professionals—doctors, lawyers, college professors. About one-fifth of them had fled Germany, fearful of the rise to power of Adolf Hitler. The Germans had a great influence on culture and society in the Jewish community. They also were relatively prosperous, and the funds they brought with them helped strengthen the economy of the Jewish community.

This heavy immigration greatly increased the Jewish population of Palestine. It grew from about twenty-four thousand people in 1882 to more than six hundred thousand people by 1948. The continuing growth pleased the Zionists, those who supported a Jewish homeland in Palestine, but began to alarm the Arabs. In time the Arabs turned from peaceful protests to a campaign of terror, riots, and pogroms against the Jews. To appease the Arabs during the time of the British Mandate, the British restricted Jewish immigration to Palestine again and again. Restrictions placed on immigration when the British controlled the area led to *Aliyah Bet*, clandestine, illegal immigration. According to the Israel Ministry of Foreign Affairs, "The period of clandestine immigration was one of the most crucial chapters in the history of the struggle for an independent Jewish state in Palestine." It proved to be the salvation of many Jews fleeing the Nazi Holocaust. Between 1934 and 1948 more than a hundred thousand Jews were brought into the country illegally.

The greatest deluge of immigrants to Israel to that point in time—688,000 people—arrived during the nation's first three years, 1948–1951. Since then many hundreds of thousands more have come, and they have changed the character of Israel yet again. Since the late

1980s around 1 million former Soviet citizens have streamed into Israel, a fair percentage of them not Jews according to religious law. Nonetheless, by the mid-1990s, more Jews had immigrated to Israel from the former Soviet Union than from any other country in the world. Today Russians constitute the largest national group in Israel. According to Dina Siegel, author of *The Great Immigration: Russian Jews in Israel*, the scale and nature of the Russian migration to Israel changed both the nation's official approach to immigration and its ideology.

At about the same time the Russians were making their presence felt in Israel, Ethiopians began entering the country by the thousands. In 1977, the prime minister of Israel, Menachem Begin, had convinced the president of Ethiopia to allow 200 Ethiopian Jews to go to Israel aboard an Israeli military jet returning to Israel. The Ethiopians were known as *falasha mura*, an ancient Jewish community who for the most part were subsistence farmers living in small villages in the mountains. From November 1984 to January 1985, a secret forty-five-day airlift through Sudan known as Operation Moses brought 8,000 Ethiopian Jews to Israel. In May 1991, the Israelis conducted another airlift, Operation Solomon, which brought another 14,200 to Israel. Since then, other Ethiopians have immigrated to Israel, and the Ethiopian community consists of about 120,000 immigrants and their descendants. The modern Israeli culture and way of life proved very different from the traditional culture and lifestyle of the Ethiopian immigrants, and they have had a difficult time adjusting. Most are not well-educated, are poor, and live in the least desirable neighborhoods. In August 2008 Israel ended its policy of immigration from Ethiopia in an effort to devote more resources to integrating Ethiopian Jews already in the country.

The efforts and determination of the early Jewish immigrants made possible the creation of the state of

Israel. Although new Jewish immigrants from different parts of the world continue to arrive in Israel, in recent years their numbers are fewer. According to an immigration ministry spokesperson, almost as many people are leaving Israel as are immigrating to it. Since 1948, all Israeli governments have made it their policy to encourage Jewish immigration for both political and emotional reasons, not the least of which is the continued survival of Israel as a Jewish nation. That policy is not expected to change.

World Map

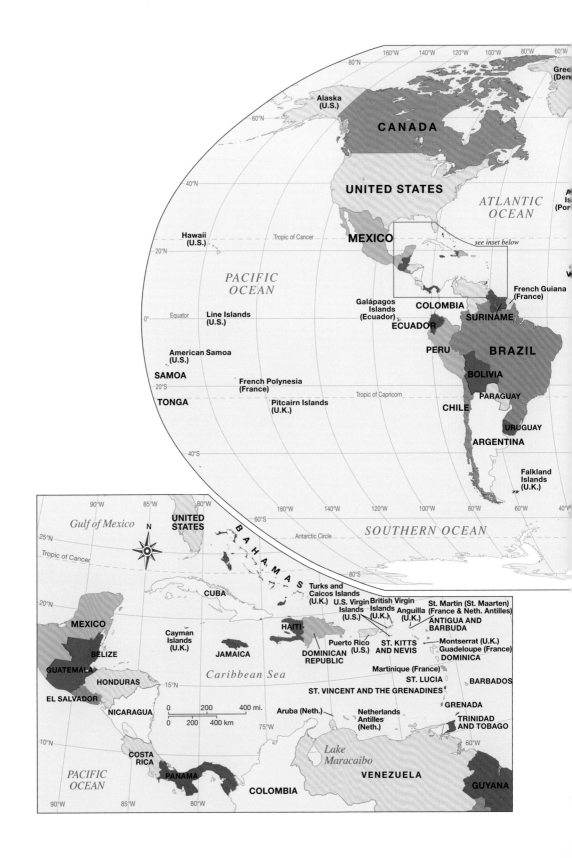

160°W 140°W 120°W 100°W 80°W 60°W

80°N

Gree
(Den

Alaska
(U.S.)

60°N

CANADA

40°N

UNITED STATES

ATLANTIC
OCEAN

A
Is
(Por

Hawaii
(U.S.)

Tropic of Cancer

MEXICO

see inset below

20°N

PACIFIC
OCEAN

V

French Guiana
(France)

Galápagos
Islands
(Ecuador)

COLOMBIA

SURINAME

0° Equator Line Islands
(U.S.)

ECUADOR

PERU

BRAZIL

American Samoa
(U.S.)

SAMOA

BOLIVIA

20°S

French Polynesia
(France)

Tropic of Capricorn

PARAGUAY

TONGA

Pitcairn Islands
(U.K.)

CHILE

URUGUAY

ARGENTINA

40°S

Falkland
Islands
(U.K.)

160°W 140°W 120°W 100°W 80°W 60°W 40°V

60°S

SOUTHERN OCEAN

Antarctic Circle

80°S

90°W 85°W 80°W

Gulf of Mexico N

UNITED
STATES

B
A
H
A
M
A
S

25°N

Tropic of Cancer

CUBA

Turks and
Caicos Islands
(U.K.)

U.S. Virgin British Virgin
Islands Islands
(U.S.) (U.K.)

Anguilla
(U.K.)

St. Martin (St. Maarten)
(France & Neth. Antilles)

ANTIGUA AND
BARBUDA

20°N

MEXICO

Cayman
Islands
(U.K.)

HAITI

JAMAICA

Puerto Rico
(U.S.)

DOMINICAN
REPUBLIC

ST. KITTS
AND NEVIS

Montserrat (U.K.)
Guadeloupe (France)

DOMINICA

BELIZE

GUATEMALA

HONDURAS

Caribbean Sea

15°N

Martinique (France)

ST. LUCIA

BARBADOS

ST. VINCENT AND THE GRENADINES

EL SALVADOR

NICARAGUA

0 200 400 mi.

0 200 400 km

75°W

Aruba (Neth.)

Netherlands
Antilles
(Neth.)

GRENADA

TRINIDAD
AND TOBAGO

10°N

COSTA
RICA

PANAMA

Lake
Maracaibo

60°W

PACIFIC
OCEAN

COLOMBIA

VENEZUELA

GUYANA

90°W 85°W 80°W

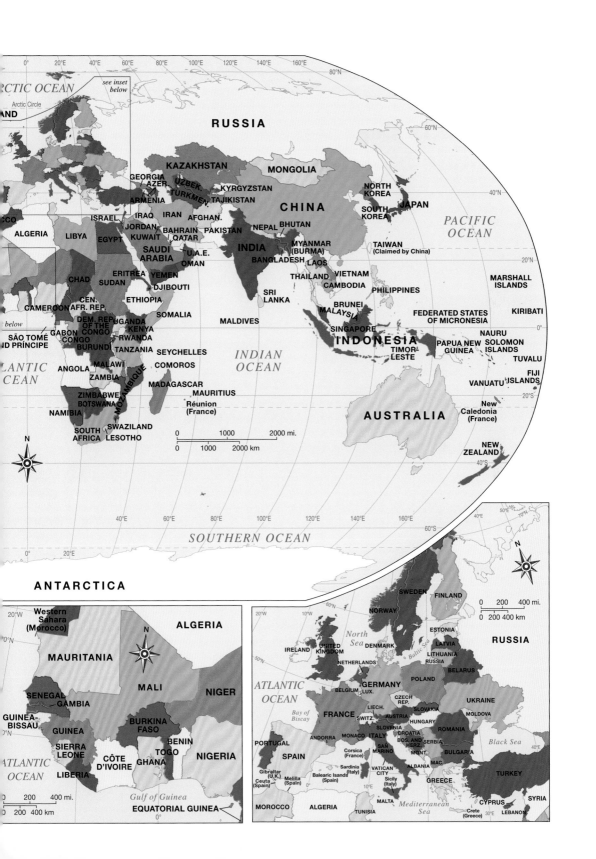

CHAPTER 1

Historical Background on the Creation of the State of Israel

From Palestine to Israel: An Overview

Sara Pendergast, Ralph G. Zerbonia, and Tom Pendergast

The following viewpoint, excerpted from Sara Pendergast, Ralph G. Zerbonia, and Tom Pendergast's multi-volume *Middle East Conflict Reference Library*, introduces and provides a brief overview of major factors that culminated in the establishment of Israel as an independent state in 1948. Heavy immigration to Israel by Jewish people seeking refuge from anti-semitism, accompanied by the rise of Zionism, played an early role. So did the Balfour Declaration, which proclaimed that the British sought to create an independent Jewish state in Palestine without taking away the rights or the privileges of non-Jewish people in the region. Other key factors followed, including the British Mandate of Palestine, the decision by the British to end their mandate in Palestine, and ultimately the division of Palestine into two separate but linked political bodies by the United Nations.

A 1909 land auction at the site that was to become Tel Aviv, Israel. The city's name came from the writings of Theodor Herzl, pioneer of modern Zionism, and means "Hill of Spring." (**AP Images.**)

SOURCE. Sara Pendergast, Ralph G. Zerbonia, and Tom Pendergast, *Middle East Conflict Reference Library*. Belmont, CA: UXL, 2006.

Palestine is a land claimed by two determined peoples, the Jews and the Arab Palestinians. . . . Both . . . feel that they were promised access to and control of this land by foreign powers that governed Palestine during the 1800s and 1900s. . . .

Reacting to violent anti-Jewish riots, or pogroms, Russian Jews began to leave their country to settle in Palestine in the late nineteenth century. The first such groups formed an organization called Lovers of Zion with Zion being an ancient name for Eretz Yisrael ["Land of Israel"]. In 1881 a Russian named Leo Pinsker wrote a book called *Autoemancipation*. According to William L. Cleveland, author of *A History of the Modern Middle East*, Pinsker's booklet "argued that anti-Semitism was so deeply embedded in European society that . . . Jews would never be treated as equals. . . . Jews could not wait for Western society to change; they had to seize their own destiny and establish an independent Jewish state."

Pinsker's book, along with the first wave of Jewish immigration to Palestine (known as the first aliyah), brought approximately thirty-five thousand Jews to Palestine. . . .

> The Jews . . . wanted more than simply an independent society within Palestine, they wanted to form an independent Jewish state.

The second wave of immigration was far more organized and determined. A Hungarian Jew named Theodor Herzl independently came to many of the same conclusions as Pinsker, and in 1896 he published a book called *The Jewish State*, which drew mass attention to the Zionist cause. Herzl argued very convincingly that Jews living throughout Europe had all the characteristics of a nation—a shared religion, history, and culture—but that they lacked a state in which they could live out their hopes and dreams for the future. . . . From 1896 on, Zionists grew ever more focused on creating a national home for Jews in Palestine. . . .

This great surge of Zionist organizing led directly to the second aliyah, which brought approximately forty thousand Jews to Palestine, mostly from Russia, between 1904 and 1914. This influx of settlers helped to establish some of the first stable and permanent Jewish social institutions in Palestine. Settlers built the foundations for the city of Tel Aviv, the first all-Jewish city. They joined together to create farms that would allow Jews to be self-sufficient, meaning that they could provide all of their own food. In 1909 they established the first kibbutz, or collective farm. . . . The Jewish people were building an independent Jewish society alongside but independent of the Arab society that already existed in the area. The Jews, however, wanted more than simply an independent society within Palestine, they wanted to form an independent Jewish state. This task was difficult to achieve without the support of either the failing Ottoman Empire, which oversaw the region, or Britain, the dominant European power in the Middle East. . . .

The Balfour Declaration

Under Ottoman rule, which had provided stability in the Middle East starting in 1516, the populations of the regions of Palestine, Greater Syria, Lebanon, and Mesopotamia (later Iraq) were left under the control of leading Arab families. As long as the families paid their taxes to the empire, the empire did not interfere greatly in their affairs, including the affairs of Jews, who began to represent a significant minority population in Palestine. But the coming of World War I brought immense change to the region. The Ottoman Empire sided with Germany in the war in the hopes of revitalizing the strength of the empire and keeping Western European powers such as France and Britain from gaining control over the Middle East.

> [The Balfour Declaration] was arguably the single most influential document in the history of the Middle East.

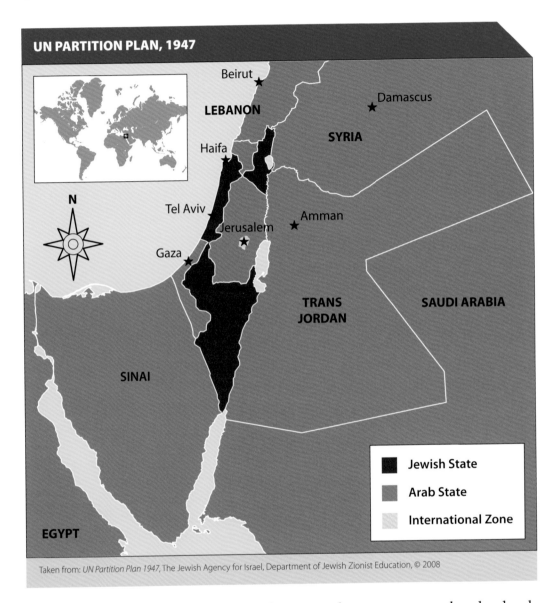

UN PARTITION PLAN, 1947

Beirut

LEBANON

Damascus

Haifa

SYRIA

N

Tel Aviv

Jerusalem

Amman

Gaza

TRANS JORDAN

SAUDI ARABIA

SINAI

EGYPT

Jewish State

Arab State

International Zone

Taken from: *UN Partition Plan 1947*, The Jewish Agency for Israel, Department of Jewish Zionist Education, © 2008

Britain and France, however, were already developing plans to defeat the Ottoman Empire. They recognized that the Arab populations in the region had legitimate claims to self-rule, and that these populations were willing to help Britain and France fight against the Ottomans. In order to encourage Arab assistance, Britain and France promised that they would help the

Arabs build independent nations. Britain was also very interested in gaining cooperation from the Jewish community in Palestine. High-placed Jews in London, especially Chaim Weizmann, a spokesman for the Zionists, convinced British diplomats that they could win the support of Russia (which encouraged Jewish immigration to Palestine) in the war if they offered support for a Jewish homeland in Palestine. . . .

> World opinion after [World War II] was in favor of granting independence to the Arab nations of the Middle East.

In order to secure all of its many interests . . . the British government in 1917 issued a brief statement known as the Balfour Declaration. In its entirety, it read: "His Majesty's Government view with favour the establishment in Palestine of a national home for the Jewish people, and will use their best endeavours to facilitate the achievement of this object, it being understood that nothing shall be done which may prejudice the civil and religious rights of the existing non-Jewish communities in Palestine, or the rights and political status enjoyed by Jews in any other country."

This statement was arguably the single most influential document in the history of the Middle East. Britain had committed itself to what would soon prove to be a nearly impossible task, creating an independent Jewish state in Palestine without taking away the rights or the privileges of non-Jewish people in the region. . . .

British Mandate of Palestine

Following World War I, the victorious Allies—Britain, France, and the United States—joined with other nations to decide the fate of the Middle East. The plan they devised . . . was called the mandate system. Under the mandate system, the Middle East was divided into territories that were expected to become independent nations. . . . France thus gained mandate power over

The corpses of Jewish men killed in a 1900 Ukrainian pogrom cover a wooden table. (Hulton Archive/ Getty Images.)

Syria and Lebanon, and Britain gained control over Iraq, Transjordan, and Palestine. The Arab nations moved relatively quickly toward independence, but Palestine soon became deeply divided between the Jewish and Arab populations.

The British mandate of Palestine began in 1920 under the supervision of Sir Herbert Samuel, an experienced British politician. . . . Britain knew that it could not ignore the Arab Palestinians in its support of the Jews in Palestine. The British . . . had pledged to cooperate with

Arab leaders to develop the economy of Palestine. Samuel also publicly proclaimed Britain's duty to live up to their promises in the Balfour Declaration to uphold the rights of Palestinians, the Arab inhabitants of Palestine that the actual declaration had characterized as the "existing non-Jewish communities in Palestine." The promises the British had made to both sides of the emerging conflict for control of Palestine made it very difficult for them to commit their resources to the support of either side. As a result Britain's support continued to shift, favoring first one group, then the other. . . .

By the late 1930s it had become apparent to all that the Jews and Arabs were not willing to live together in Palestine. In 1937 the British Peel Commission Report called for Palestine to be partitioned, or split, into independent Arab and Jewish states. Jews considered this solution, but wanted to modify it; Arabs rejected it outright, declaring that giving land to an outside minority was an unjust solution. . . . In 1939 the British tried again, issuing a policy paper, called the White Paper, that . . . proclaimed that Britain no longer planned that Palestine would become a Jewish state and announced further limits on Jewish immigration to Palestine. . . .

The events of World War II brought about major shifts in power, both in the Middle East and in the rest of the world. Three of these shifts are particularly important for understanding politics in Palestine. First, the war exhausted Britain and, as the war came to an end, the British looked for ways to withdraw from [their] commitment to administer Palestine. Second, world opinion after the war was in favor of granting independence to the Arab nations of the Middle East. The Arab League, a coalition of Arab nations formed in 1945, was especially sympathetic to the desire of Arab Palestinians for their own nation. Finally, the world's horror at Hitler's "Final Solution," the ghastly name given to his attempt to exterminate all European Jews, created a great sym-

> "The state of Israel was now a reality, recognized by the United Nations and welcomed by many in the international community."

pathy, especially in the United States, for the creation of a Jewish state in Palestine. . . .

In February 1947 Britain requested that the United Nations come to Palestine to provide assistance. By August of that year the United Nations Special Committee on Palestine (UNSCOP) called for an end to the British mandate and for the partition, or division, of Palestine into two separate but linked political bodies. The British announced in September that they would end their mandate by May 14, 1948. . . .

The partition plan was voted on and passed in the United Nations on November 29, 1947, marking the first time that the international community publicly endorsed the idea of a Jewish state. . . .

The Arab-Israeli War

From the moment that UNSCOP announced its plan of partition in 1947, the situation in Palestine changed from one in which politicians lobbied to win support for their land claims to one in which armed groups fought with each other to secure land. This scramble to claim land and define boundaries occurred in two distinct phases: the first in what has been called the Intercommunal War, when Jews and Palestinians fought among themselves, and then in the first Arab-Israeli War (called the War for Independence in Israel) in which the neighboring Arab nations fought to deny Israel its independence. . . .

Unwilling to supervise the partition plan, British forces left Palestine on May 14, 1948, and on that same day David Ben-Gurion [Israel's first prime minister] proclaimed the existence of the state of Israel roughly within the borders defined by the United Nations partition plan. The next day, the armies of Egypt, Iraq, Lebanon, Syria, and Transjordan invaded Israel. . . .

The fighting in this war was largely over by August 1948. Israeli forces not only secured the areas granted by the United Nations partition, they also significantly expanded Israeli-controlled territory in the north, capturing the entire northern quarter of Palestine all the way to the Lebanese border, and making real gains on both the northern and southern edges of the West Bank, a Palestinian-dominated territory west of the bank of the Jordan River. . . . By the middle of 1949, Israel had negotiated ceasefire agreements—though not peace treaties—with all its neighboring countries, and considered its borders secure and established. The state of Israel was now a reality, recognized by the United Nations and welcomed by many in the international community.

Israel had secured a victory and realized the Zionist dream, but in so doing, it had also created significant regional problems. The first and biggest problem was that of Palestinian refugees. . . .

Another significant problem created by Israel's rise to independence is the lasting ill will and anger that it created among Arab nations. Arab nations would fight a series of wars with Israel over the next thirty years and would consistently deny Israel's right to exist.

Reactions to the 1947 UN Approval of Partition

The Economist

In the following viewpoint, the British newspaper *The Economist* contends that while Jewish people are accepting of the United Nations 1947 approval of the partition for Palestine, the Arab population is defiantly opposed. For the most part, the new Jewish state is united and working hard to resolve internal political situations, the lack of room for all the immigrants seeking immediate entry, and other problems. The Arab population does not want to recognize the partition: They want the Jewish people out of Palestine and are willing to resort to violence to achieve their goal. The Arab state is in denial and refuses to make plans to take over and administer the Arab part of the country.

The reaction of the three interested communities in Palestine to the United Nations' approval of partition has been almost exactly what one

SOURCE. The Economist Special Correspondent, "Partition on the Spot," *The Economist*, December 13, 1947, pp. 963–964. Copyright © 1947 The Economist Newspaper Limited. Republished with permission of The Economist Newspaper Limited.

would have expected. The Jews are pleased, the Arabs angry, and the British sceptical. But sentiments stop short of excess. There were frenzied Jewish rejoicings; now many Jews are finding imperfections in the plan. There were widespread Arab riots; they were neither as violent nor as lengthy as many officials expected. The average British official (the adjective is carefully chosen) first said, "The whole thing's damn silly"; on reflection his attitude is more, "Well, it's an admirable scheme on paper, but . . ."

Partition is a victory for the Jewish people, and was celebrated as such. But some of their leaders realise already that, unless they walk extremely warily, victory may be costly and its fruits bitter. It has already created new and difficult problems. The Zionist movement has in the past maintained surprisingly strict discipline

Egyptians gather in Cairo's Opera Square in 1947 to protest the United Nations' partition of Palestine and to hear speeches by Arab leaders, who can be seen atop the structure to the right. (**AP Images.**)

> **It will be an authoritarian and ruthless state; but it will work.**

amongst its adherents, most of whom are not by nature disciplined people. Now there is a slight cracking of that discipline. There is an immediate demand both from would-be immigrants waiting in Europe and also from lands where, in the past, Jews seemed reasonably secure, that the gates of Palestine be at once opened to them. But no appreciable increase in immigration is likely until the British administration is withdrawn; even when the Jews take over their part of Palestine it will still not—they say—be possible to bring in more than a maximum of 5,000 a month. So the Jewish Agency, or the Jewish Government, will soon be appreciating some of the difficulties which for so long bedevilled the British.

Fears of persecution have led Jewish communities settled for generations in the Moslem countries of the Middle East and North Africa to send urgent appeals to the Agency that they should be immediately brought to Palestine. "We are hostages: our lives are in danger," is the tenor of the messages. This problem the Agency had not foreseen. They fully intend that at some future date these Middle East Jews should emigrate to Palestine (whether they want to or not), but there is no room for them yet; priority must be given to European Jews. . . .

A Complex Government

The new Jewish State faces even more complex internal situations, of which the most important are political. The executive of the Jewish Agency which, until a constitution is promulgated and elections held, will probably turn itself into a temporary government, is composed of nineteen members. Eight of them belong to the General Zionists, seven to Mapai (Palestine Workers' Party) and four to the strict orthodox Mizrahi Party. Seats are held in the Asefath Hannivharim (the elected assembly) and indeed on other representative bodies such as the Va'ad

Leumi (national council) much in the same proportion, but with the addition of representatives of half a dozen smaller parties. Since the United Nations decision, two of these parties, the left-wing Socialists and left-wing Labour, both previously against partition and anti-Mapai, have announced their readiness to accept partition and to work with Mapai. This makes Mapai now far stronger than the General Zionists and can give official Jewish policy a strong leftish tendency.

The Mapai leaders, David Ben Gurion, chairman of the Agency Executive, Mosche Shertok and Mrs Golda Meyerson, are probably delighted with this development on a long-term basis. For immediate purposes, however, they are playing it down. They are at pains to point out that "Jewish Socialism" will be "for internal consumption only," and that they have no thought of any general "socialisation" of Jewish economy. This disclaimer is clearly aimed at pacifying their wealthy American supporters, who might be alarmed—and stop the flow of dollars—if they thought action would be taken in Jewish Palestine against private capital.

Incidentally, it has not yet been decided what name the new Jewish State will adopt. Zion is a popular suggestion; but, some Jews point out sadly, "you can't have a Zionist State, call it what you will, that doesn't include the city of Zion—Jerusalem." Eretz Israel, Israel, Palestine are other possibilities.

Faced though they are by these and a multitude of other problems, the Jews are exerting all their boundless energy and initiative—and, in financial matters, their guile—in hastening the construction of their state. It will be an authoritarian and ruthless state; but it will work.

Arabs Without a Plan

What can one say about the Arab State? The Palestine Arab leaders—the Mufti and the members of the Arab Higher Executive—know that unless they can reverse the United Nations decision by force of arms, partition will be inevitable. Yet they still refuse even to consider making plans to take over and administer their part of the country. Further, they refuse to allow any of the more reasonable, progressive young Arabs, who realise that something has got to be done, to make any plans of their own. The surprisingly complete observance of the three-day protest strike called by the Mufti shows that the Arabs follow the Mufti's orders. They dislike having the Jews in their "own land" and would be delighted to turn them out by force. But no Arab with his senses about him can believe that to be physically possible until, at any rate, very considerable assistance is furnished by the Arab States. It would, therefore, have seemed reasonable to make some attempt to keep what they have and to maintain their part of Palestine as a going concern, which it is, thanks to a maligned British Administration and also to Jewish initiative and Jewish money.

> There will be the very reverse of good will from the Arab side, and so it is possible that the 27-year-old conflict will continue.

Nothing of the kind has happened. So far as can be seen, there will be no authority, no administration, not even leaders, to whom the departing British or the United Nations Commission can formally deliver the deeds of Arab Palestine. As transfer of authority must be made, opinion in British circles here is tending more and more to the idea of giving King Abdullah of Transjordan the baby to hold.

The Odds of Success

Can partition succeed? With good will on both sides the answer is obviously "yes." It is not an ideal solution: but it could be a solution and no one has produced a better or even a workable alternative. Unfortunately, there will be the very reverse of good will from the Arab side, and so it is possible that the 27-year-old conflict will continue—

without a British administration to hold the ring and take the blame. The Jews will make a most determined effort to make a success of their state; Jewish leaders who had for years set their faces against partition have now accepted it *faute de mieux* [for lack of anything better]. The danger is—if the Arabs finally accept the solution— that the Jews might use their state as a stepping off ground for peaceful penetration of the rest of Palestine. Jewish voices have already complained that partition violates their historical conception of a Palestine "on both sides of the Jordan." The extremists of the Revisionist Party and the terrorist organisations are for that reason flatly against it. Among even moderate Zionists there is equal determination that, come what may, Jerusalem must be returned to the Jews.

How implacable the Palestine Arabs' opposition to the division of "our own country" will remain depends mainly on the attitude of the neighbouring Arab States. Nationalism has a firm hold on the Moslem countries, but their dependence upon the Western Powers is still a factor capable of bringing about surprising changes in policy, which in their turn may alter the ideas of the Palestine Arabs.

The Future of Israel after the British Mandate Ends

The Times of London

The following viewpoint from the May 12, 1948, edition of the British newspaper *The Times of London* details the British plans for withdrawal from Palestine as the British Mandate in that country comes to an end. The overriding concern is what will happen when the British no longer are in charge. Arabs and Jews must cooperate to ensure progress made during the mandate is not lost and that institutions established are maintained and continue to grow. A lack of Arab leadership threatens the future of an independent Arab Palestine, and strong Arab hostility and escalating attacks threaten the very future of the new Jewish state and make the already daunting task of the Jewish people all the more difficult.

SOURCE. "Last Days in Palestine," *The Times*, May 13, 1948, p. 4. Copyright © 1948 Times Newspapers Ltd. Reproduced by permission.

When the British mandate in Palestine ends and the Arabs and Jews are left alone together a Zionist State will for all practical purposes come into being. How the two peoples will fare, whether the Jewish State will be formally as well as informally established, and whether it will endure are questions for the future to answer. If the Arab States and the Arab inhabitants of Palestine remain hostile and continue the struggle, if there is sabotage, boycott, and massacre, the Jews will require all their strength to survive as a State.

The proposed terms of a truce for Jerusalem that were sent by the High Commissioner to the Arabs and Jews have now been made public, no reply from either having been received. They provided for a cessation of hostilities, the entry of supplies under impartial control, free access for Jews to the Old City and the Wailing Wall, and evacuation of Katamon [neighborhood in south-central Jerusalem] by the Jews.

> 'Until we succeed in securing the good will of the Arabs a dark portentous shadow remains over the National Home.'

Many people now regard the Arabs as being in the same position as the Russians aganst Napoleon and Hitler, and if the issue remains a military one the comparison is apt. The Arabs have by nature the long view; it remains to be seen whether they have tenacity of purpose and the ability to find civilian and military leaders, now lacking, to turn their fortunes.

One of the Jews has truthfully written: "Until we succeed in securing the good will of the Arabs a dark portentous shadow remains over the National Home." The Jews may stand squarely on ground possessed by force, having still the authority of the United Nations' adoption of partition [in November 1947] behind them, but with an unfriendly Arab world around them their State cannot settle down to an orderly existence.

> Leaders must emerge, or else the independent Arab Palestine will disintegrate.

British Inroads Must Be Kept Alive

Jubilant though they are, many Jews realize this. The influx of capital from abroad and skill of organization will not permanently solve the problem of this small State in coping almost at once with the nearly 30,000 refugees now in Cyprus and perhaps a minimum of 100,000 more from Europe. These are crucial factors, though the ability of the Jews to master them should not be underestimated.

There is much, however, to which Jew, Arab, and Briton have put their hands, sometimes jointly. The sense of regret, and frustration almost, which many British officials have felt on leaving may be tempered if they consider the moderately good progress made in education, labour, civil aviation, broadcasting, agriculture, public works, and the judiciary.

It will now fall to the Jews and the Arabs separately to keep these branches alive. The Jews, if they are not engaged unduly in fighting the Arabs or in curbing those whom they euphemistically call dissidents—already there has been an exchange of kidnapping between the Hagana [Jewish defense force] and the Irgun [Zionist terrorist group] in Haifa—will undoubtedly do so, with perhaps the autocratic hand they have already shown in defence matters. How the Arabs will manage is more uncertain, but a nucleus of trained workers is at hand. Leaders must emerge, or else the independent Arab Palestine will disintegrate.

The British Withdrawal

The Government announced that, as the mandate legally ends at midnight between Friday and Saturday, the High Commissioner will leave Jerusalem on Friday for Haifa and sail at midnight in H.M.S. *Euryalus*. The post-mandate withdrawal of troops from Jerusalem and Palestine will

also begin on Friday, and presumably the remaining British officials will leave Jerusalem the same day.

To-night the G.O.C. [general officer commanding] proclaimed the area that his troops will occupy in withdrawing from Palestine. This area will be under his military jurisdiction, and is, roughly, the long coastal strip from south of Acre to the Egyptian border, except the towns from Jaffa to Nathanya. Any interference with the troops or their communications or stores will be severely punished, but the inhabitants will not otherwise be interfered with. Military courts and a British police force will be at work in the area. The port of Haifa and the railways will be under commanders appointed by the G.O.C.

The Jews to-day reported that the Arab Legion was using Bren carriers and that infantry were attacking the Kfar, Etzion group of settlements south of Jerusalem. Of the road to Jaffa the Jews are saying little, and two cor-

Members of Haganah, the Jewish Agency defense organization, escort three Palestinian Arabs who have been expelled from Haifa. (AFP/Getty Images.)

respondents to-day found the road clear for about 15 miles down to the second water pumping station at the Jerusalem end of the Bab el Wad. Below this point firing sounded in the hills, and the Jews declared they had been shelled half an hour before.

Three Days of Turmoil in Palestine's History

The Jerusalem Post

The following viewpoint from the May 16, 1948, edition of *The Jerusalem Post* details events in and concerning "Jewish Palestine" over a three-day period beginning May 14 with the proclamation by the head of the provisional government, David Ben-Gurion, of the establishment of the State of Israel. The United States gave de facto recognition to the new state, Russia and its allies said they intended to give their recognition as well, but the United Nations faltered. All of Jewish Palestine, meanwhile, was in a state of blackout, bombs were dropped on the city of Tel Aviv, a cease-fire petered out, and a battle raged for control of Jerusalem.

For the Jewish population there was the anguish over the fate of the few hundred Haganah [Jewish defense organization] men and women in the Kfar Etzion bloc of settlements near [the city of] Hebron.

SOURCE. "Most Crowded Hours in Palestine's History," *Jerusalem Post*, May 16, 1948. Copyright © 1948 Jerusalem Post. Reproduced by permission.

Their surrender to a fully equipped superior foreign force desperately in need of a victory was a foregone conclusion. What could not be known, with no communications since Thursday morning, was whether and to what extent the Red Cross and the Truce Consuls would secure civilized conditions for prisoners and wounded, and proper respect for the dead. Doubt on some of these anxious questions have now been resolved.

On Friday afternoon, from Tel Aviv, came the expected announcement of the Jewish State and its official naming at birth, "Medinat Yisrael"—State of Israel, with the swearing in of the first Council of Government. The proclamation of the State was made at midnight, coinciding with the sailing from Haifa of Britain's last High Commissioner. Within the hour, President [Harry] Truman announced in Washington that the Government of the United States had decided to give de facto rec-

Israel's first prime minister, David Ben-Gurion (left), on May 15, 1948, stands with an official who displays the signed document proclaiming the establishment of the Jewish State of Israel. (AP Images.)

ognition to the Jewish State, with all that such recognition implied. The Assembly of the United Nations, meeting since the middle of April for "further study" of the Palestine problem was thus left, by one means or another, to ratify the Two-States decision of November [1947], or dissolve with nothing concrete to its credit. The Assembly adjourned with the resolution to appoint a mediator between the Jews and Arabs, to cooperate with the Security Council's Truce Commission in Jerusalem.

> "The members of the Arab League completed their plans for a full-scale invasion of Palestine in what has been described as a Moslem 'crusade' against the Jews."

Russia and her allies had given early assurance of their intention to recognize the Jewish State, whoever else did or did not. As a result of Washington's action and the Eastern Bloc's stand, other countries are expected to extend their recognition to the newly born state.

An Arab Invasion

Nor did the Arab Bloc remain idle. True to promises, or threats, the members of the Arab League completed their plans for a full-scale invasion of Palestine in what has been described as a Moslem "crusade" against the Jews. Tel Aviv was bombed twice yesterday by Egyptian war planes. One of the enemy planes was shot down by a Jewish fighter plane, and the pilot taken prisoner, showing that this move against the civilian population was not a surprise, and that the Jewish preparations include anti-aircraft defences.

A black-out has been ordered for the whole of Jewish Palestine. Tel Aviv itself having blacked out on Friday.

At the same time, the air was filled with reports of two Egyptian columns on the move from the south towards Gaza and Beer Sheba, and of intensified shelling from across the northern border of Jewish settlements in North Eastern Galilee.

David Ben-Gurion: Israel's First Prime Minister

The son of a lawyer, David Gruen was born on October 16, 1886, in Plonsk (Czarist Russia; now Poland). He received a traditional Jewish education, later adding some secular studies in Warsaw. In 1900 he was among the founders of the Zionist youth club Ezra; in 1903 he joined the Zionist socialist movement, Poalei Zion.

Gruen arrived in Palestine in September 1906. He changed his name at that time to the Hebraic David Ben-Gurion, after a defender of Jerusalem who died in 70 A.D. Zionism and socialism were both seen by the young Ben-Gurion as necessities for the future of the Jewish people. To him Zionism meant the obligation to come to Palestine, settle the land, and use Hebrew as everyday speech.

By 1947 he was a major spokesman for the Zionist cause before the United Nations Special Committee on Palestine, which later that year proposed the partition of Palestine and the formation of a Jewish state. As the British mandate was about to expire, Ben-Gurion proclaimed the restoration

The Security Council met yesterday in a special session to consider action on the invasion of Palestine by member states of the U.N.

In the afternoon, Jerusalem was subjected to shelling from the northwest. Haganah forces throughout the country continued mopping up, and Jewish sources claimed most of Western Galilee safe against attack. Naharayim, near Jist el Majamie, inside Trans-Jordan, where the Jordan river works of the Palestine Electric Corporation are, is claimed by the Arab Legion. The battle for the Tel Aviv-Jerusalem Road at Bab el Wad is still on, Haganah taking two villages—Abu Shusha and Kubab—between [the two cities of] Ramleh and Latrun.

An Ongoing Battle for Jerusalem

In Jerusalem the "cease fire" observed on both sides for six days was broken on Friday, although the more stra-

of the state of Israel on May 14, 1948.

Serving as prime minister and minister of defense from 1948 to 1963 (except for a brief retirement from 1953 to 1955), Ben-Gurion revealed himself to be not only an astute party leader but also a great statesman. He protected Israel from invasion by establishing a well-equipped and well-trained people's army. He forged the image of Israel as a modern democratic country based on parliamentary rule, a unique sociological and political phenomenon in the Middle East. During his premiership more than a million Jews, from 80 countries and speaking many languages, came to Israel. The absorption and integration of the immigrants and the Israeli achievements in housing, agricultural settlement, employment, industry, education, health services, and trade, under the Ben-Gurion government, were among the remarkable accomplishments of the twentieth century.

Ben-Gurion died December 1, 1973.

tegic buildings in Princess Mary Avenue, the Russian Compound, and Jaffa Road passed to the Jews without a shot being fired, as did the David Building commanding the road to the German Colony and Railway Station. By yesterday evening, Jewish forces were approaching some of the gates of the Old City. The Police Training School on Mt. Scopus and Sheikh Harrah are in Jewish hands.

On Friday morning, the Truce Commission met at the French Consulate and invited Jewish and Arab representatives to confer with them. Jewish Agency delegates agreed that the "cease fire" be extended in Jerusalem for eight days. Arab representatives could not attend, they said, because of the firing in Julian's Way, and a two-hour respite was arranged from 5 to 7 in the evening. Whether they agreed or not, became academic as by that time the battle for Jerusalem had been renewed.

To Jerusalem's tension was added the aggravation of electric power failing in most parts of the city, as nearly all of the Electric Corporation's lines had been shot down. This meant, on top of the other hardships to a fuel-less city, no broadcast news yesterday, when there were no newspapers. For more than a week the city was also without piped water.

Israel Becomes a State

The Jerusalem Post

The following viewpoint from the May 16, 1948, edition of *The Jerusalem Post* documents the speech given by David Ben-Gurion, head of Israel's newly formed Provisional Council of Government, proclaiming the creation of *Medinat Yisrael*, the State of Israel. Ben-Gurion affirms the historic and national rights of the Jewish people to a Jewish state. The new state will welcome Jewish immigrants from all countries; safeguard the Holy places of all religions within its borders; afford full freedom of religion, culture, and language; and work for the economic union of Palestine as a whole. Ben-Gurion reaches out to the Arabs of Palestine, asking Arab citizens to return to their homes, stop the bloodshed, and restore peace to the land.

T he first act of the Council of Government, as announced by its head, was to abolish all legislation of the 1939 White Paper of the late Mandatory Power, particularly the Ordinances and Orders relating to immigration and land transfer.

SOURCE. "Proclamation by Head of Government," *Jerusalem Post*, May 16, 1948. Copyright © 1948 Jerusalem Post. Reproduced by permission.

Mr. [David] Ben Gurion prefaced the declaration with a review of the historic connection of the Jewish people with the land of Israel and of their efforts to return, which never ceased throughout the generations of their dispersal, until the Nazi holocaust proved anew the urgency of the need for a Jewish State.

The Balfour Declaration of 1917, confirmed by the League of Nations, had given explicit international recognition to the right of the Jewish people to reconstitute its National Home in Palestine, he said.

"On November 29, 1947," continued the declaration, "the United Nations decided on the establishment of a Jewish State and an Arab State in Palestine and called upon the inhabitants of the country to take all steps necessary for the establishment of two States.

> Pursuant to the decision of the U.N. and based on our historic and national rights, we hereby declare the establishment of the Jewish State which will be called "Medinat Yisrael" (State of Israel).

"This decision cannot now be changed. Accordingly, we, the mem-

APPROXIMATE POPULATION CHANGE IN MANDATORY PALESTINE, 1922–1947

Year	Source	Muslim % of Total	Jewish % of Total	Christian % of Total	Other % of Total
1922	Census	78.34	11.14	9.50	1.01
1931	Census	73.52	16.90	8.60	0.98
1937	Estimate	63.32	27.91	7.94	0.83
1945	Survey	58.35	32.96	7.86	0.84
1947	Projection	58.06	33.24	7.86	0.84

Taken from: www.mideastweb.org/palpop.htm

bers of the Provisional Government Council, members as we are of the Jewish Agency for Palestine, and representatives of the entire Jewish Community in Palestine, are meeting on this historic day when the British Mandate comes to its end.

Jewish immigrants arrive in Israel only days after the new nation's establishment. (AFP/Getty Images.)

"Pursuant to the decision of the U.N. and based on our historic and national rights, we hereby declare the establishment of the Jewish State which will be called 'Medinat Yisrael' (State of Israel)."

"This State will be provisionally governed by this Council acting as a Provisional Government Council and taking over its duties at midnight, on May 15 with the end of the [British] Mandate."

"This Provisional Government Council will function until due governmental bodies have been constituted by a newly elected Constituent Assembly, which shall meet not later than October 1, 1948."

"The Provisional Government Council will be the Provisional Government of the State of Israel until the elected Constituent Assembly meets."

Open Gates to Immigration

"The State of Israel will open its gates to immigration of Jews from all lands. It will strive to develop the country for the benefit of all its inhabitants, in accordance with the social ideals of our Prophets."

"We declare that full civil and political liberty will be enjoyed by all citizens, regardless of religion, race, or sex. There will be full freedom of religion, culture and language."

"We declare that we shall safeguard the Holy Places of all religions within the area of the State of Israel."

"We declare our readiness to cooperate closely with all relevant bodies of the U.N. in accordance with the resolution of November 29, 1947."

"We declare our readiness to work for the economic union of Palestine as a whole."

A Call for Peace and Support

"We call upon the U.N. to give its blessing to the establishment of the Jewish State, to help us in our efforts and to accept the Jewish State into the family of nations."

"Even at this hour of bloodshed, we call upon the Arabs of Palestine to restore peace in this country. We call upon the Arab citizens to return to their homes. We assure them full civil rights on the basis of full representation in all governmental organs of the State. We are extending the hand of friendship to the neighbouring Arab states in order to initiate mutual cooperation. We are ready to contribute our share to the revival of the Middle East."

"We call upon the Jewish people in all lands of its dispersion to stand fast and lend us every support in our struggle for the establishment of the State of Israel."

Mr. Ben Gurion then announced that those members of the Provisional Council who were in Jerusalem and unable to reach Tel Aviv in time for the meeting, had met in Jerusalem on Friday morning and had notified their colleagues in Tel Aviv that they joined in the declaration.

"In virtue of this authority," Mr. Ben Gurion then said, "the Provisional Council of Government is established."

Israel Is a Model of Instant Democracy

I.D.W. Talmadge

In the following viewpoint, written in 1948, journalist I.D.W. Talmadge maintains that four months after Israel was proclaimed a state, its government is the most stable regime in the Middle East. He contends that the government has achieved such success because it is democratic and has the unwavering support of the people. A foremost principle of a new special Ministry of Minorities is encouragement of self-governing institutions among the Arab population. Talmadge maintains that the new state is every bit as socialist as England. The Histadrut, the General Federation of Jewish labor, controls almost one-fourth of the economy and most agriculture is owned jointly by members of a group rather than by any individual. At the time this viewpoint was written, I.D.W. Talmadge was the foreign affairs editor of *Scholastic* magazine.

SOURCE. I.D.W. Talmadge, "Israel: The Making of a State," *The Nation,* September 25, 1948, pp. 337–339.

The state of Israel, unlike Rome, was built in a day. Within twenty-four hours after the British pulled out, the Jews had a fully functioning state. They had a Cabinet and a Provisional Parliament. From nowhere they produced an army, an air force, and even a sizable naval fleet. Before the last Tommy [British soldier] had stepped aboard the last ship for England, an effective Jewish government was in operation—complete from Prime Minister down to sanitation inspector.

Overnight a new, prefabricated structure of administration was erected. Jewish personnel moved in and took over the offices and bureaus vacated by the British. Essential government services were hardly interrupted. Everything went off smoothly as planned. The schools opened as usual, the buses ran on time, the mail was delivered on schedule. The hospitals, the factories, the telephone exchange—all continued to work as if nothing had happened.

Only, where the Union Jack [British flag] flew the day before, the new standard of the Republic of Israel was unfurled. And the signs on the government buildings were repainted in Hebrew characters. A new seal bore the inscription "Medinat Isroel"—"State of Israel." By the next day the new-born state even had its own postage stamps.

Today, four months later, that hastily installed government is still functioning. It is, indisputably, the most stable regime in the Middle East. It has survived the armed attack of six sovereign states. The secret of its success is simple. The government of Israel is a democratic government receiving the unswerving support of the people.

Democracy Is Key

There is amazingly little red tape and even less pomp and protocol. Members of the Cabinet work in their shirt sleeves, without ties. At first there was too much informality. People would drop in to have a *schmüss* [talk] with Prime Minister David Ben-Gurion or Foreign

Golda Meir: Israel's Fourth Prime Minister

Golda Meir was Israel's fourth prime minister, serving from 1969 until her resignation in 1974. She was the only woman to head the state of Israel and one of a handful to have led modern nations. When people would ask Meir, who had a reputation for toughness, if she felt handicapped at being a woman minister, she would reply: "I don't know. I've never tried to be a man."

Golda Mabovitch was born May 3, 1898, in Kiev, Russia, to a poor Jewish family. The family immigrated to the United States in 1906. During her teens, while living with her parents in Milwaukee, Wisconsin, and her sister, Sheyna, in Denver, Colorado, she came into contact with numerous socialist Zionists and joined Poalei Zion (Workers of Zion) in 1915. With the November 1917 passage of the Balfour Declaration, in which Sir Arthur Balfour committed the British to the support of the creation of a Jewish homeland in Palestine, she decided to immigrate to Palestine, persuading her new husband, Morris Meyerson, with whom she later had two children, to join her.

After the formation of the state of Israel in 1948, Meir became Israel's first ambassador to Moscow but was

Minister Moshe Shertok and suggest to them how to run the government. That had to be stopped. But even today a session of the Provisional Parliament resembles a meeting of the executive board of a trade union more than of a national legislative body.

Fourteen political parties, including the puny Communist Party, are represented in the Provisional Parliament, or State Council. The Communists have one representative among the thirty-seven members. As one legislator explained to me, "We can't give them less than one seat." It is not uncommon for the Prime Minister to be outvoted in the Israeli Parliament. But as becomes a democratic leader of a democratic state, Ben-Gurion takes it graciously. Even in war time Israel is not a dictatorial state. Any suggestion of totalitarianism is repug-

called back to join the Knesset (parliament) after seven months. During her tenure as labor minister from 1949 to 1956, Meir's main responsibility was overseeing the assimilation of Jewish immigrants, tens of thousands of whom were then living in tent cities.

In 1956 she became foreign minister. David Ben-Gurion, who was then prime minister, persuaded her to take on the Hebrew-sounding name Meir. During her decade-long tenure as foreign minister, Meir pursued a close relationship with the United States and gained significant quantities of arms from it.

In March 1969, following the death of Levi Eshkol, Meir became prime minister. Again, she focused on keeping arms flowing from the United States and resisting initiatives to negotiate with the Palestinians. During this time numerous Jewish settlements were set up on the newly occupied West Bank and Gaza Strip.

Meir, an unassuming and down-to-earth politician, was accused by her opponents of being stubborn and unsophisticated. Her supporters cherished her warmth and simplicity. She died in Jerusalem on December 8, 1978.

nant to the Jewish masses. Accordingly, strikes were not outlawed despite the desperate struggle for national survival.

I talked with an official of the Ministry of Police. "The outgoing government can scarcely be said to have handed over to us any central police organization," he told me. But by the end of [August 1948] about 100 officers, 70 N.C.O.'s [noncommissioned officers] and 1,300 men had been trained and posted. "The Israeli police is still at less than half strength," this official continued. "For example, the department cannot provide more than twelve men for night patrol in all of Tel Aviv. It is noteworthy, however, that crimes of violence in Israel are some 30 per cent lower than they were a year ago in the towns and 50 per cent lower in the rural areas."

No Gap in Financial Functions

The Israeli Ministry of Finance took over the financial functions of the state without any gap or hitch—an achievement which would have been astonishing even had there been sympathetic cooperation from the outgoing authority. As a result of careful preparation beforehand, income tax, customs, and excise duties were collected without interruption. Even in the first crowded days the Ministry initiated action in fields where the Mandatory Government had been in default. Immediately after the declaration of the Israeli state a national loan was launched for 5,000,000 Palestinian pounds. This loan has already been subscribed.

A special Ministry of Minorities was set up in the Cabinet under the able leadership of Behor Shitreet. Its purpose is to defend the interests of the Arab and Christian minorities in Israel and to promote friendly relations among the three religious communities. One of its main principles is the encouragement of autonomous institutions among the Arabs. Arab schools have been reopened. An Arab newspaper is now published in Israel. Even during the fighting the Israeli government appointed Arabs to police Arab areas in Palestine.

> [The new state of Israel] . . . is certainly as Socialist as Australia or New Zealand or England itself.

Separation of Synagogue and State

In the new state of Israel synagogue and state are separate and will continue to be so under the proposed constitution. Saturday is the day of rest instead of Sunday—and that's about all that makes Tel Aviv any different from an American city. Synagogue attendance in Israel is about as good, or bad, as church attendance in America. Dietary laws are not universally observed. Some restaurants serve *kosher* meals, others don't. The story is told—it is probably apocryphal—that the Arabs, who are not permitted to eat pork, raise hogs to sell to their Jewish neighbors.

A draft constitution for the state of Israel is patterned on the American model and guarantees freedom of expression, worship, assembly, and association. The preamble to the proposed basic law of Israel asseverated [declared] that "the state shall insure the sanctity of human life and uphold the dignity of man." An interesting innovation in the projected constitution is a clause which provides that freedom of expression shall not be accorded to movements which advocate the suppression of the democratic form of government. Among provisions being considered for inclusion are guaranties for a national system of compulsory unemployment, old-age, and health insurance; equal pay for men and women; prohibition of child labor; and minimum hours of employment for women in industry.

A Socialist State

Israel is the most eastern of the Western democracies. Its destiny is in the hands of a party (the Mapai) which is the very counterpart of the British Labor Party. . . .

How Socialist is the new state of Israel? It is certainly as Socialist as Australia or New Zealand or England itself. The bus you board in Tel Aviv or Haifa, the Tnuva restaurant where you eat, the shop where you buy your clothes, the factory where the clothes are made are for the most part owned by the Histadrut, the General Federation of Jewish Labor. And so are the leading bank and the largest insurance company. In fact, the Histadrut controls almost a fourth of the national economy. Its membership comprises nearly half of the adult population.

Moreover, most of the country's agriculture is collectivized. In the *kibbutzim* (farming communes) all property is owned in common and all members contribute and share alike. . . . There is no coercion in the communes, no party functionaries to lay down the "line," no

Allied Arab forces behind a barricade fire on Jewish fighters of the Haganah, the self-defense force of the Jewish Agency, in the city of Jerusalem. (**AFP/Getty Images**.)

threats of imprisonment or exile. One is free to join or quit a commune at will. . . .

Socialist labor dominates the government and its institutions only by virtue of its electoral strength. It has not set up a dictatorship of the party. There are no fewer than twenty-five political parties in tiny Israel. The strongest of these is the Mapai. . . .

[About fifteen parties] are represented in the thirty-seven-man Provisional Parliament. . . .

Not participating in the government are two dissident groups—the Irgun Zvai Leumi and the Fighters for Freedom of Israel (the Stern gang). The Irgun claims a following of 6,000 and the Stern organization claims about 1,500. Both groups plan to take part in the coming electoral contest. . . .

The infant state of Israel is the youngest member in the family of nations. To the amazement of its United Nations nursemaids, it has turned out to be a tough kid, with a tenacious will to live.

CHAPTER **2**

Controversies Surrounding the Creation of the State of Israel

The Jewish People Deserve a Home

A.J. Balfour

In the following viewpoint, a speech made to the British House of Lords in 1922, A.J. (Arthur James) Balfour argues that the Jewish people have made major contributions in almost all aspects of society and have earned the right to a Jewish homeland. The British Mandate of Palestine, he contends, will give the Jewish people the opportunity to have a home in which they can, under British rule, develop their culture and traditions free from the persecution they have had to endure for centuries. A.J. Balfour was a British politician and statesman who served his country in many capacities, including prime minister (1902–1905) and foreign secretary (1916–1919). In 1917, he wrote the Balfour Declaration, a controversial statement recognizing the Jews' right to a homeland in Palestine.

Photo on previous page: An unidentified Israeli official and a Haganah military policeman grip their newly proclaimed nation's flag as they prepare to raise it over the Haifa Airport. (**AP Images.**)

SOURCE. A.J. Balfour, *Penguin Book of Twentieth Century Speeches.* London, United Kingdom: Viking Penguin, 1999. Copyright © 1992, 1993, 1999 Brian MacArthur. All rights reserved. Reproduced by permission of the Literary Estate of Earl Arthur James Balfour.

My noble friend [John Dickson-Poynder, Lord Islington] told us in his speech, and I believe him absolutely, that he has no prejudice against the Jews. I think I may say that I have no prejudice in their favour. But their position and their history, their connection with world religion and with world politics, is absolutely unique. There is no parallel to it, there is nothing approaching to a parallel to it, in any other branch of human history. Here you have a small race originally inhabiting a small country, I think of about the size of Wales or Belgium, at any rate of comparable size to those two, at no time in its history wielding anything that can be described as material power, sometimes crushed in between great Oriental monarchies, its inhabitants deported, then scattered, then driven out of the country altogether into every part of the world, and yet maintaining a continuity of religious and racial tradition of which we have no parallel elsewhere.

> [The Jewish people] have been able, by this extraordinary tenacity of their race, to maintain this continuity, and they have maintained it without having any Jewish Home.

Jewish Contributions Deserve Recognition

That, itself, is sufficiently remarkable, but consider—it is not a pleasant consideration, but it is one that we cannot forget—how they have been treated during long centuries, during centuries which in some parts of the world extend to the minute and the hour in which I am speaking; consider how they have been subjected to tyranny and persecution; consider whether the whole culture of Europe, the whole religious organization of Europe, has not from time to time proved itself guilty of great crimes against this race. I quite understand that some members of this race may have given, doubtless did give, occasion for much ill-will, and I do not know how it could be otherwise, treated as they were; but, if you are going to lay stress on that, do not forget what part they have played in the intellectual, the artistic, the philosophic and scientific development of the world. I say nothing of the economic side of their energies, for on that Christian attention has always been concentrated.

I ask your Lordships to consider the other side of their activities. Nobody who knows what he is talking about will deny that they have at least—and I am putting it more moderately than I could do—rowed all their weight in the boat of scientific, intellectual and artistic progress, and they are doing so to this day. You will find them in every University, in every centre of learning; and at the very moment when they were being persecuted, when some of them, at all events, were being persecuted by the Church, their philosophers were developing thoughts which the great doctors of the Church embodied in their religious system. As it was in the Middle Ages, as it was in earlier times, so it is now. And yet, is there anyone here who feels content with the position of the Jews? They have been able, by this extraordinary tenacity of their race, to maintain this continuity, and they have maintained it without having any Jewish Home.

> We should then have given [the Jews] what every other nation has, some place, some local habitation, where they can develop the culture and the traditions which are peculiarly their own.

British Mandate Gives Jews a Home

What has been the result? The result has been that they have been described as parasites on every civilization in whose affairs they have mixed themselves—very useful parasites at times I venture to say. But however that may be, do not your Lordships think that if Christendom, not oblivious of all the wrong it has done, can give a chance, without injury to others, to this race of showing whether it can organize a culture in a Home where it will be secured from oppression, that it is not well to say, if we can do it,

that we will do it. And, if we can do it, should we not be doing something material to wash out an ancient stain upon our own civilization if we absorb the Jewish race in friendly and effective fashion in these countries in which they are the citizens? We should then have given them what every other nation has, some place, some local habitation, where they can develop the culture and the traditions which are peculiarly their own.

I could defend—I have endeavoured, and I hope not unsuccessfully, to defend—this scheme of the Palestine Mandate from the most material economic view, and from that point of view it is capable of defence. I have endeavoured to defend it from the point of view of the existing population, and I have shown—I hope with some effect—that their prosperity also is intimately bound up with the success of Zionism. But having endeavoured to the best of my ability to maintain those two propositions, I should, indeed, give an inadequate view to your

While visiting Jerusalem, British foreign secretary Arthur Balfour points out a feature of the Church of the Holy Sepulchre to the city's governor, Ronald Storrs. Jerusalem's Arab populace was on strike as a protest against the 1917 Balfour Declaration, which supported creation of a Jewish homeland in Palestine. (Topical Press Agency/Hulton Archive/ Getty Images.)

Lordships of my opinions if I sat down without insisting to the utmost of my ability that, beyond and above all this, there is this great ideal at which those who think with me are aiming, and which, I believe, it is within their power to reach.

A Worthwhile Experiment

It may fail. I do not deny that this is an adventure. Are we never to have adventures? Are we never to try new experiments? I hope your Lordships will never sink to that unimaginative depth, and that experiment and adventure will be justified if there is any case or cause for their justification. Surely, it is in order that we may send a message to every land where the Jewish race has been scattered, a message which will tell them that Christendom is not oblivious of their faith, is not unmindful of the service they have rendered to the great religions of the world, and, most of all, to the religion that the majority of your Lordships' House profess, and that we desire to the best of our ability to give them that opportunity of developing, in peace and quietness under British rule, those great gifts which hitherto they have been compelled from the very nature of the case only to bring to fruition in countries which know not their language, and belong not to their race. That is the ideal which I desire to see accomplished, that is the aim which lay at the root of the policy I am trying to defend; and, though it be defensible indeed on every ground, that is the ground which chiefly moves me.

The British Plan to Partition Palestine Is Not the Best Solution

Herbert Samuel

In the following viewpoint, Herbert Samuel describes the situation in Palestine that has prompted the British to send a commission of inquiry to investigate. The report presented in 1937 by the commission proclaims that the current partition and mandate are not working. Palestine should be divided into three parts—a new Jewish state, an Arab section to be united with an existing principality, and a neutral section under British control. Samuel contends that even though partition is not a good solution it is the only probable one so long as the Arab population and the Jewish people show no willingness to cooperate with each other. Samuel was a British statesman and philosopher. In 1909 he became one of the first Jewish members of the British cabinet. In 1920 he was appointed the first British high commissioner for Palestine, a position he held for five years.

SOURCE. Viscount Herbert Samuel, "Alternatives to Partition," *Foreign Affairs*, vol. 16, October 1, 1937, pp. 143–155. Copyright © 1937 by the Council on Foreign Relations, Inc., www .ForeignAffairs.com. Reproduced by permission.

When the representatives of a war-weary world met at Paris in 1919 the problem of Palestine seemed one of the simplest of the many that confronted them. Turkey made no claim for the retention of her sovereignty. The system of Mandates was established with general approval, and Palestine was obviously a case for its application. As to the choice of a Power as Mandatory, there was only one candidate. Great Britain was willing to accept the duty. . . .

The Zionist Movement, which for thirty years had been struggling, slowly and painfully, to found colonies of Jews in Palestine in the face of stolid Turkish obstruction, now took a leap forward. Year after year, with immense energy, the Zionists collected funds from their co-religionists all over the world. They bought land, trained young men and women as colonists, organized emigration from the crowded and often unfriendly countries of Europe to the promised land, so old and so new, that was at last opened to them. . . .

During the seventeen years that have since elapsed a considerable part of the cultivable land of Palestine has passed into Jewish ownership, bought, often from absentee landlords, at prices many times its previous value. The Jewish population of Palestine has risen from some 60,000 to over 400,000. . . .

A Growing Arab Nationalism

But meanwhile there had also been growing a movement of nationalism among the Arabs. Simultaneously with the striking progress of the Zionist Movement, a spirit of Arab patriotism, previously almost non-existent in Palestine, had arisen. . . . Those in Palestine looked upon themselves as an outpost of the Arab world, specially charged with the guardianship, within the old city of Jerusalem, of one of the three most

> 'It is impossible, we believe, for any unprejudiced observer to see the National Home and not to wish it well.'

sacred shrines of Islam. They viewed with apprehension the Jewish incursion (for so it appeared to them) and feared that at no distant date they would be swamped altogether by it. . . .

As a result of the nationalist movement among the Arabs, disorders had broken out on a small scale as early as 1920, and on a somewhat larger scale in 1921. Then for a period of eight years there was tranquillity, though there continued to exist an undercurrent of political tension. In 1929 serious and widespread disturbances occurred in many parts of the country, resulting in some hundreds of deaths. Finally in 1936 disorders broke out again, and lasted for many months, reaching almost the dimensions of a rebellion and requiring the dispatch of two divisions of British troops to Palestine.

> 'The answer to the question "Which of them [Jews or Arabs] in the end will govern Palestine?" must surely be "Neither."'

Public opinion in Great Britain had by this time become seriously perturbed, and the Government determined to review the whole situation. The first stage was to order a thorough inquiry into the facts. . . .

Six Commissioners were appointed; their competence and impartiality were acknowledged on all hands. They went to Palestine; spent several weeks in visiting all sections of the country and in hearing the views of all parties; and on June 22, 1937, presented a unanimous Report. . . .

The British Dilemma Regarding Palestine

The Commissioners speak in most appreciative terms of the work already accomplished by the Jews in Palestine. They write: "It is impossible, we believe, for any unprejudiced observer to see the National Home and not to wish it well. It has meant so much for the relief of unmerited suffering. It displays so much energy and enterprise and devotion to a common cause." They praise highly its achievements, both economic and cultural. And they declare, repeatedly and with emphasis, that the Arabs have greatly gained in a material sense from the Jewish immigration. While the Jewish population has grown since the Mandate by 350,000, the Arab population has increased by exactly the same figure. Nevertheless, the conclusion reached by the Royal Commission is pessimistic. On the political side they consider that the problem as hitherto presented is insoluble. "The obligations Britain undertook towards the Arabs and the Jews some twenty years ago . . . have proved irreconcilable, and, as far ahead as we can see, they must continue to conflict. . . . We cannot—in Palestine as it now is—both concede the Arab claim to self-government and secure the establishment of the Jewish National Home." Yet neither of these aims can be discarded. "Arab aspirations towards a new age of unity and prosperity in the Arab world" are legitimate and praiseworthy; to those aspirations "British public opinion is wholly sympathetic." On the other hand, it is out of the question that, having encouraged the intense Jewish effort in Palestine by assurances of the most formal character, Great Britain should now merely wash its hands of the whole matter and discard responsibility. "Manifestly," the Commissioners say, "the problem cannot be solved by giving either the Arabs or the Jews all they want. The answer to the question 'Which of them in the end will govern Palestine?' must surely be 'Neither.' We do not think that any fair-minded statesman would suppose, now that the hope of harmony between the races has proved untenable, that Britain ought either to hand over to Arab rule 400,000 Jews, whose entry into Palestine has been for the most part facilitated and approved by the League of Nations; or that, if the Jews should become a majority, a million or so of Arabs should be handed over to their rule."

Need for a Wholly Different Plan

The Commission criticizes some aspects of the British administration of the country. . . .

The Commission imply in their Report that the fomenters of the disturbances of 1936 had been allowed too much scope. . . .

The Commission are inclined to criticize also the choice of officials for the British service in Palestine. . . .

But the Commissioners are clearly of the opinion that, even if all those things had been different, even if none of these mistakes had occurred, the underlying problem would have remained. There would still have been the essential antagonism, as they regard it, between the Jewish aims and the Arab aims, and still the impossibility of finding any policy, along the lines hitherto pursued, that would end it. So they have devised a wholly different plan, not previously advocated in any quarter. Their proposal is a division of the country into three parts: a new Jewish state; an Arab section which would be united with the existing Arab Principality of Trans-Jordan; and a neutral section which would remain under the administration of Great Britain as mandatory. . . .

The British Government, simultaneously with the publication of the Report, declared its general acceptance of these recommendations. It announced that it would forthwith approach the League of Nations with a view to the ending of the present Mandate, and the

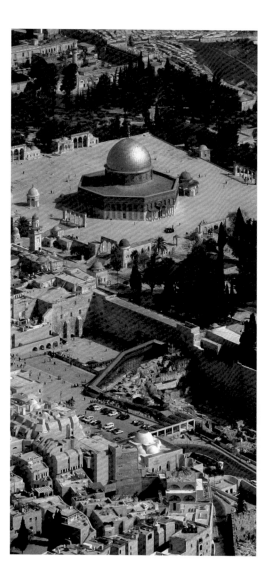

Known to Jews as the Temple Mount, the Dome of the Rock is at the heart of the Israeli-Palestinian conflict. (AP Images.)

> The scheme of partition . . . is subject to grave objections.

substitution of a new one on the lines proposed. Meanwhile Great Britain would continue to bear responsibility for the government of Palestine; if serious disorders should again break out, martial law would be declared; land sales by Arabs to Jews would be restricted during the period of transition; Jewish immigration would only be allowed to continue at a rate not exceeding in any circumstances the figure, suggested by the Commission, of 12,000 a year.

The declaration of the British Government was prompt, definite and uncompromising. Nevertheless it did not command general acquiescence. . . .

A Proposed Alternative

As the only member in either House [of Parliament] who had held the post of High Commissioner for Palestine, it fell to me to take part in the debate in the [House of] Lords and to offer an examination of the conclusions of the Royal Commission. I could not but agree with their judgment that it was necessary to make a fresh start. Undoubtedly the present situation is a deadlock. . . .

The scheme of partition, however, is subject to grave objections. It does not effect, and no scheme of partition possibly could effect, a clear severance between the Arab and the Jewish populations of Palestine: the geographical conditions do not allow it. . . .

I ventured to suggest an alternative plan: not to end the existing Mandate, not to regard as altogether hopeless the policy of coöperation, remembering that since peace and tranquillity had reigned for eight years it was not impossible that it might be restored, though on a new basis. The alternative might embrace five points: First, a recognition by the Jews that they must make some sacrifice in order to reassure the Arabs and arrive at a reconciliation; and this sacrifice should take the form of a limitation of the Jewish population of Palestine, during a period of years, to an agreed percentage of the whole. (I suggested, tentatively, forty percent; the present percentage is about thirty.) Secondly, the aspirations of Arab nationalism should be recognized and should be assisted, and efforts made to promote the formation of a great Confederation in the Middle East, in which Palestine should be included, to which it would bring wealth, and in which the industries of Palestine would find a vast and valuable market. Thirdly, Trans-Jordan should be opened by agreement to the settlement of both Jews and Arabs, and a loan arranged to promote that object. Fourthly, the ownership of the Moslem Holy Places in Palestine should be guaranteed by the League of Nations in perpetuity. Fifthly, the Jewish Community in Palestine as now organized, and the Arab Community, provided with a new organization, should each be given large powers over the education of their own peoples and over public health and other matters, and be provided with adequate revenues from taxation. A new Advisory Council should be established, in which each Community would be represented as such; the Council should also contain the principal British officials: it would be consulted by the High Commissioner on all matters of common concern. I agreed that, if Jews and Arabs did not come to an agreement on some such basis as this, the only alternative would be to face partition with all its disadvantages and risks.

> " No one is enamored of the solution by partition. Its difficulties and dangers are recognized on all hands. "

A Plan in Flux

In the House of Commons matters took an unexpected turn. . . . The Government had given notice of a motion approving the recommendations of the Royal Commission and their own acceptance of them; but this

The Role of the Western Wall

For those who follow the Jewish faith, the western wall of the Judaic Temple complex is believed to be closest to the site in the inner sanctuary where the Ark of the Covenant and its Ten Commandments were kept. This site in the Temple is known as the Holy of Holies, and consequently, the Western Wall has become a popular destination for visitors and prayers. Some Muslims also believe the site to be holy because it was the spot where the prophet Muhammed tethered his winged steed, Buraq, on his way to Heaven.

On August 14th and 15th, 1929, in the midst of long-standing Arab-Israeli polarization concerning territory in Jerusalem and the surrounding areas, Jewish activists staged demonstrations in Tel Aviv and at the Western Wall in Jerusalem. On August 16th, following rumors that these same activists planned to claim holy places in Palestine as well, Muslims demonstrated by burning Jewish offerings at the Wall. During the course of violence instigated in part by these demonstrations, 133 Jewish and 116 Arab people were killed in August 1929 alone; and hundreds more were injured.

Violence erupted again in the Arab-Israeli War of 1948, and Jordan captured East Jerusalem, barring Jewish access to the Wall for 19 years. But in 1967's Six-Day War, the Jewish population reclaimed Jerusalem and its holy landmark. Now the Wall looks out on an adjacent plaza that accommodates its daily visitors of diverse faiths, who come to be near the venerable site and to leave prayers written on scraps of paper in the Wall's cracks.

motion was subjected to vigorous criticism. . . . It was urged that the Government were acting too hastily; that the plan of partition raised very grave issues, and, even if accepted in principle, might have to be modified in many points of application; time should be given for the reactions of both the Jews and the Arabs to be ascertained. Ultimately these views carried the day. . . .

At the time when this article is being written the whole matter is under the consideration of the Congress which is the final authority in the Zionist Movement; of the two sections of the Palestine Arabs . . . and of the Permanent Mandates Commission of the League of Nations. . . .

No one is enamored of the solution by partition. Its difficulties and dangers are recognized on all hands. The Royal Commission would undoubtedly have preferred to recommend an alternative based upon coöperation between the two parties if they had regarded such coöperation as a possibility. It cannot be doubted that the British Government would still welcome that solution if it were attainable. But whether either of the parties directly concerned would consent to such a sacrifice of its particular aims as would be necessary to win the assent of the other party, is very doubtful. Both dislike the very idea of the partition of Palestine, but neither shows—as yet—any sign of such a change of attitude as would permit an escape from that drastic solution.

British Obligations to the Jewish People Are Not Legal

Higher Arab Committee

The Higher Arab Committee argues in the following viewpoint from 1938 that the proposed British partition of Palestine was biased in favor of the Jewish people at the expense of the Arab population. British obligations to the Jewish people are unjust and based on force and evil and, therefore, are not legal, the committee argues. The committee contends that the British must accept the Arabs' national program, which includes recognition of Palestine as an independent Arab country. The Higher Arab Committee was formed in British Mandatory Palestine in 1936 by six prominent Arab leaders. Headed by the Grand Mufti of Jerusalem, Haj Amin al-Husayni, its mission was to protest British support of Zionist progress in Palestine. The committee led a campaign of Arab revolt against Jewish and British targets.

SOURCE. Higher Arab Committee, "Statement by the Higher Arab Committee 1938," *National Archives, U.K.*, 1938, pp. 182–188, document reference FO 684/11. Copyright © 2005 The National Archives, London. Reproduced by permission.

The Partition Commission's report constitutes the worst possible end to the unsuccessful policy of sending commissions. It is regrettable and incomprehensible that a report of this nature should consider Palestine, which is already a Holy Place, and the heart of the Arab homeland, and which moreover is but a small country, as a fit object to be divided, torn, cut up, and parcelled cut. The British commission came with this theory in mind but was brought to a standstill when attempting to fix boundaries; we consider therefore its new partition scheme still-born, the more so that the British Government after careful perusal of the report have concluded that the establishment of two nations in one country was impracticable.

The Arab Committee deeply regrets that so long a time was required for His Majesty's Government to realize this truth which was obvious from the very first day; and we ask ourselves with pain who is responsible for the misfortunes which have fallen on the country on account of the Government policy—a policy which has ended in the failure of the partition scheme—and who is responsible for the destruction which has been inflicted on the country in pursuance of this policy. Will Palestine continue to be threatened by similar dangerous programmes evoked by the dreams of Zionists and colonizers, which the British Government will set out to fulfil? The idea of granting to the Jews a right in Arab Palestine and of instituting a National Home for them in the heart of the Arab homeland gave rise to the policy of partition which has had so unfortunate an ending. All things based on wrong are wrong; and any future scheme to benefit the Jews at the expense of the Arabs will meet with the same fate.

> [The Arab people] hope that the British Government realize also that the scheme was not equitable and have definitely abandoned the idea of partition in any form.

The Impracticality and Unfairness of Partition

As regards the British Government's statement (of policy) the Arab people note with pleasure that Great Britain has abandoned the partition scheme and has realized that partition was impracticable; and they hope that the British Government realize also that the scheme was not equitable and have definitely abandoned the idea of partition in any form or of any of these schemes similar to partition which were at one time under discussion.

> The Arab people cannot consider British obligations to the Jews, which are based on force and evil, as a fundamental . . . of the Palestine question.

The Arab people also note with pleasure that the British Government have adopted a method of negotiation and have realized that the Palestine question should be solved by political, as opposed to military, means; they note also with pleasure the envisaged collaboration of the Arab nations towards a settlement of this question which has dragged on for so long. They consider this as an admission that the Palestine question is a general Arab question. The Higher Arab Committee is, however, astonished at and disapproves of Syria and the Lebanon being excluded from the negotiations, despite their close relations with Palestine, on a pretext that they are under mandate, while the Government of Transjordan, which is also under mandate, has been asked to take part.

Arab Denial of British Obligations

The Highest Arab Committee disagrees with the statement of the British Government that "they are faced with a problem of finding alternative means of meeting the difficult situation which will be consistent with their obligations towards Arabs and Jews", because they do not admit the legality of British obligations to the Jews, these obligations being based on force and hostility and being at the expense of others. The Royal Commission stated in its report, and the British Government and the British delegates to the League of Nations have confirmed, that British obligations to Jews and Arabs were contradictory and irreconcilable; the attempt now once again to reconcile these contradictory obligations can lead to no result, and to base the solution of the question on such a reconciliation is impracticable and can only lead to new difficulties. The Arab people cannot consider British obligations to the Jews, which are based on force and evil, as a fundamental either of the Palestine question or of the proposed negotiations.

The British Government state that the surest foundation for peace and progress in Palestine would be an understanding between Arabs and Jews. The Higher Arab Committee consider that such an understanding is irrealisable so long as the Jews persist in their wrongful ambitions in Palestine. If, by an understanding, the British mean that the Jews may live in peace amongst the Arabs, this is practicable for the Jews, and forms a part of the national program of the Arab people who alone are the owners of their country. But the claims of the Jews in Palestine are false, based only on dreams and unsupported except by British bayonets. The question should be determined by considerations of right and equity only.

An Approved Arab Program

The British Government announce their intention of inviting representatives of the Palestinian Arabs and of the Arabs from neighbouring countries to London to discuss future policy in Palestine, without defining the basis of these discussions. The Higher Arab Committee state in this connection that they have a programme which may be summarized as the complete stoppage of Jewish immigration and the replacement of the mandatory system by a treaty giving the country an independent national government. This programme has been approved by the Arab delegations, commissions, and

> If the British seriously wish to settle the question, let them face realities and declare their acceptance of the Arab programme as a basis for the proposed settlement.

governments, and the Arabs cannot renounce it for it is the sole guarantee of their existence and of their legal right to their country. It is inspired by this legal right and contains the maximum concessions to the Jews.

When negotiations are to take place to settle a question, it is customary to define the basis of negotiation, especially in cases like that of Palestine where the Jews are inspired by their dreams and rely on blind force and false propaganda. The Higher Arab Committee much regrets that the British statement contains no grounds for hope or optimism and feels that this lack of definition may result in the failure of the conference and that this may be their intention, so that the British Government may propose a policy of their own which would cause the present state of affairs in Palestine to continue. But as regards the British Government's invitation to discuss future policy the Arab people cannot regard the Jews as a party to the affair and will not enter into discussion with them as regards a solution.

The British Burden of Responsibility

His Majesty's Government reserve the right to refuse to receive those Arab leaders whom they regard as responsible for the campaign of assassination and violence. The Committee repeats, as it has many times done before, that the responsibility for the disorders from first to last belongs to the British Government and their representatives in Palestine. The Arab people only ask for their rights in their own country and it is the British authorities who have at every stage attacked in an endeavor to crush the Arabs and have closed their ears to their demands. It is therefore inequitable to hold the Arabs or their representatives responsible for the disorders which

were forced on them because the British Government had left no other means open to them of protesting against their wrongful policy—a policy which consists in imposing the Jews on them so that the Arabs were bound in the end to find themselves turned out of their own country.

Members of the Arab Higher Committee, circa 1935, following a meeting at which the group decided to boycott the Royal Commission in Jerusalem. (Keystone/ Getty Images.)

The Committee Represents Arabs

The Committee wonders on the other hand which Palestinian Arabs the British Government means if they do not refer to the members of the Committee. The British Government are fully aware that the Higher Arab Committee enjoys the complete confidence of the Arab people, and entrusts them with the task of defending Arab rights and of carrying out their programme, and that there are no others in Palestine who can pose as representatives of the Arabs in this matter. The British Government know also that any other Palestinians who accepted their invitation would not enjoy the confidence of the Arab people, nor would they truly represent them; and the Committee considers that this statement will add further difficulties to the question. The Committee considers that the British Government in making this statement, have proved that they do not wish Palestine to be properly represented in these talks, on which its very existence depends. Events in Palestine have proved that this method is already wrong.

If the British seriously wish to settle the question, let them face realities and declare their acceptance of the Arab programme as a basis for the proposed settlement, stop Jewish immigration during the negotiations, withdraw their accusations, and allow the Arabs the right to choose the representatives they trust.

The British Government declare that if the London discussions fail, they will take their own decision. The Committee points out that these reservations increase the existing difficulties. If the negotiations fail, the responsibility would be that of the British and of the Jews. The Committee proclaims to the world, from now, that in case this occurs the Arab people will be unable to accept a solution imposed on them by blind force, and which would not give them their rights, and will in any case go on enjoying the sympathy and approval of both Arab and Moslem worlds, until they will get their full rights.

The Only Road to Settlement

The Higher Arab Committee thinks it wise to take this opportunity to repeat their national programme, which is as follows:

1. Recognition to the Arabs of their right to full independence in their country.

2. Abandonment of the attempt to institute for the Jews a National Home.

3. Termination of the British Mandate and its replacement by a treaty similar to the Anglo-Iraqi, the Anglo-Egyptian, and the Franco-Syrian treaties, under which Palestine would become an independent country.

4. Complete stoppage of Jewish immigration and of sale of land to the Jews.

The Arabs are prepared to institute negotiations with the British on a legitimate basis, with the object of reaching an agreement which would safeguard reasonable British interests, and would guarantee the Holy Places and access to them, and the protection of all legitimate rights of Jews and other minorities in Palestine.

Palestine Should Not Be Partitioned

Jamal el-Husseini

In this 1947 speech to the UN General Assembly's Committee on Palestine, Jamal el-Husseini argues that Palestine should not be partitioned. He contends that all of Palestine must be returned to its rightful owners, the Arab people. The Balfour Declaration, on which the Jewish people base their claim to establish a Jewish home, is an immoral, unjust, and illegal promise made by the British, who did not own Palestine and have no right to give it away. Jamal el-Husseini was a Palestine Arab leader and nationalist who, in 1947, was chairman of the Palestine Arab delegation to the United Nations. The cousin of the grand mufti of Jerusalem, he served as prime minister of the 1948 Government of Common Palestine, which was never recognized by the United Nations.

SOURCE. Jamal el-Husseini, "Palestine Partition Denounced," *Vital Speeches of the Day*, vol. 14, October 15, 1947, pp. 2–10. Reproduced by permission.

The Palestine Arab case is simple and self-evident. . . . It hardly needs elaboration. . . . It is that of a people who desire to live in undisturbed possession of their country, in which they have continually existed and with which they have become inextricably interwoven. . . .

We have one glaring, all-embracing fact: That we are there and have always been there in actual possession of our own country, and we have one binding, lawful and sacred duty: To defend it against all aggression. We ask for no favors and we desire nothing that is not ours by birthright.

The Zionists are conducting an aggressive campaign, in fact, an invasion. For no matter with what apparel it is clothed, religious, humanitarian, or political, the Zionist movement for the possession of Palestine is nothing but an invasion that aims, by force, at securing and dominating a country that is not theirs by birthright.

The Case in a Nutshell

On one side, therefore, there is self-defense; on the other side, an aggression. . . . This is the case before you in a nutshell.

Investigation and fact-finding should have, by all means, been set afoot a long time ago, with the Zionist invaders who carry out this act of aggression and with Great Britain who enforces it at the points of their bayonets. . . .

Our rights and patrimony have been the subject of close scrutiny and investigation for not less than eighteen times in twenty-five years. During the last eighteen months alone, our case has been examined in its minutest detail four times before commissions of inquiry and at official conferences. All to no purpose. . . .

> Great Britain . . . has never owned Palestine to dispose of it.

The Balfour Declaration Must Go

The Zionists claim the establishment of a Jewish national home by virtue of the Balfour Declaration. Great Britain, however, has never owned Palestine to dispose of it. It occupied Palestine in the name of the Allies with whom the Arabs were associated. . . . When the British Army entered Palestine, the United Kingdom declared to the world that they entered it as liberators and not as conquerors.

The Balfour Declaration that contradicts the Covenant of the League of Nations, and is now standing between democracy and the Holy Land, is an immoral, unjust and illegal promise. It is immoral because it was made behind the back of the inhabitants of the country, and was diametrically opposed to previous pledges given to them by the same government. It is unjust, because it aims at the national destruction of a friendly people. It is illegal because it was a gift that was not the property of the giver. . . .

The Balfour Declaration, therefore, and its incorporation in the mandate, must be doomed as the most wicked and inapplicable policy that ever existed. If justice is to be done, it must go. . . .

Great Britain, as one of the greatest powers, and the Zionist organization, the most influential association in the capitals of the world, have joined hands, thirty years ago, to execute a policy in Palestine that aims at the destruction of the national existence of its Arab owners.

In 1918, when this policy of wholesale destruction was set afoot, Palestine was 93 per cent Arab in population, language, traditions and aspirations. This overwhelming, all-prevailing Arab atmosphere was to be overturned for the establishment of the Jewish forthcoming national home. . . .

In 1920 a draft mandate, for Palestine, again behind the back of the indigenous population, was laid down by both the Zionist executive and the British Government, and instantly put into effect. In 1922, under the influence of both, this mandate was ratified by the League of Nations without any alterations, again in the absence of the Arab owners of the country and in the face of their never-failing protests.

Article 22 of the Covenant of the League of Nations defined the objects of the mandatory system. The first paragraph of that Article states that the rights and interests of the indigenous population under the mandate become a sacred trust of civilization in the hands of the mandatory, and Paragraph 4 gives those territories that were detached from Ottoman rule, Palestine obviously included, the distinctive position in which they will enjoy independence, subject, temporarily, to administrative advice and assistance by mandatory.

The Palestine mandate, as ratified, corresponds neither to the first paragraph nor to the last. For its object is to create a home for a people who were not in Palestine, and who have no direct relation with the indigenous population. . . .

What is known as the Palestine Administration has no relation to the people, in the sense that it represents London and not Palestine. The inhabitants of Palestine, and the Government which they were supposed to constitute and for whose assistance the British Government got the mandate, have no place or existence in this British combination.

The present administration of Palestine consequently has no legal basis under the Government of the League of Nations. . . .

Arabs Have No Rights or Freedoms in Palestine

As far as political freedom is concerned, the Arabs, contrary to the letter and spirit of Article 22 of the Covenant of the League of Nations, have no existence in Palestine.

> The Arab world is a racial homogeneity.

We have no say whatsoever in the administration. We have no say in legislation. We have no responsible positions. We have no control over or knowledge of the external or internal policy of the Government. Our political existence as indigenous population whose rights are held in sacred trust of civilization by Great Britain has thus been liquidated. . . .

This policy has cost all concerned, including the mandatory, worries and losses in life and property.

The British Are Responsible

Several and successive disturbances took place, the last of which continued from 1936–39. This led the British Government, in 1939 . . . , to come to the conclusion that Jewish immigration must stop, and Palestine should, in a fixed period of time, become an independent unitary state under a constitution to be formulated by the people of Palestine. Again under Zionist pressure, the British Government did not implement that policy, but gradually backed out.

This state of affairs has created an atmosphere which augurs of calamitous developments for Palestine and the Middle East. Under the stress of these circumstances and gloomy forebodings, the British Government at last came out with the truth that the mandate was incompatible and so it was unworkable. . . .

The British Government which made the Balfour Declaration in 1917, and those who laid down the draft mandate in 1920, cannot but have realized the obvious fact that both contained inconsistent and opposed terms and as such they could not be fairly and squarely applied. . . .

They created the problem which has led to the present crisis. They ask us now to be objective and realistic, they would have us accept the position as it stands. In other words, they ask us to compromise our country and future. . . .

Arabs Are One People Worldwide

Palestine is a tiny country of only 10,000 square miles, more than half of which is uncultivatable. It has no raw materials or industries, and so it cannot afford relief for millions of Jews in distress.

The Zionist organization does not want Palestine for the permanent solution of the Jewish problem or the relief of the Jews in distress. They are after power, they are after the central and strategic position of Palestine. . . .

Their movement is . . . not one caused by distressful conditions, but it is one of political ambitions and designs on Palestine and the Near East.

This brings us to another consideration which is of fundamental importance to us, not only as Palestinian Arabs, but as Arabs of the very core of the Arab world. The Arab world is a racial homogeneity that extends over the southern and parts of the eastern border of the Mediterranean Sea from the North of Africa throughout Egypt to the Persian Gulf and from the Turkish borders to the Indian Ocean.

The people of that vast territory speak one language and have the same history, traditions and aspirations. Their unity in all these matters is bound to be a basis for mutual understanding and a solid foundation for peace in one of the most central and sensitive areas of the world.

With these characteristics, the Arab world affords a conspicuous contrast to the nations that occupy the northern border of the Mediterranean. From the Iberian Peninsula to Turkey, the different nationalities and non-homogeneous communities have clashed in a diversity of interests, mentalities and national aims. This condition created always an atmosphere of antagonism that culminated in many a calamitous war. . . .

Arabs are Entitled to a Free and Independent State

It is illogical . . . that the United Nations, the peace-making machinery of the world, should associate itself or lend a helping hand to weaken or to break up an existing natural old homogeneity as that of the Arab world by the introduction in its midst of an alien body as is now being contemplated by sponsors of a Jewish state in Palestine.

If such a political monstrosity is carried out, no sane person could expect to see peace prevail in that part of the world. . . .

It may be asked, what then is your proposal for the solution of the problem that was created by the Balfour Declaration and the mandate. . . .

The solution is in your Charter. . . . In accordance with this Charter, the Arabs of Palestine, who constitute the great majority, are entitled to a free and independent state.

[In mid-October 1947] the honorable delegate of the United Kingdom declared that his Government has come to the conclusion that the mandate for Palestine should now be terminated, and that such a termination should be followed by independence.

The Arab delegation heartily welcomes this belated declaration and trusts the British Government, this time, will not reverse its decision. . . .

With regard to the manner and form in which the independence of Palestine should be shaped, the view of the Palestine Arab delegation is that this is a matter for the rightful owners of this country to decide. The future government of Palestine cannot be imposed from without.

Once Palestine is found to be entitled to its independence, the

> The Arabs of Palestine are . . . solidly determined to oppose, with all the means at their disposal, any scheme that provides for the dissection, segregation or partition of their tiny country.

United Nations is not competent and cannot legally dictate to it the form of its government. This would amount to interference in the internal affairs of that country. The future government of Palestine must be a government by the people and for the people.

The only just, practical and democratic way to achieve the independence of Palestine is to recognize the following principles as the basis for its future constitutional organization:

1. That an Arab state in the whole of Palestine be established on democratic lines.

2. That the said Arab state of Palestine will respect human rights, fundamental freedoms and equality of all persons before the law.

Amir Faisal al Saud II of Saudi Arabia, center, confers with delegates from Iraq and Egypt—Abdullah Damlougi (left) and Abdelmonem Mostafa—who were affiliated with the Arab League to press the Palestinian case during the United Nations meeting at Lake Success, New York in 1947. (Keystone/Getty Images.)

3. That the said Arab state of Palestine will protect the legitimate rights and interests of all minorities.

4. That freedom of worship and access to holy places will be guaranteed to all.

The following steps will have to be taken to give effect to the aforesaid principles:

A. A Constituent Assembly should be elected at the earliest possible time. All genuine and law-abiding nationals of Palestine will be entitled to participate in the elections for the Constituent Assembly.

B. The said Constituent Assembly shall, within a fixed time, formulate and enact a Constitution for the Arab state of Palestine, which should be of a democratic nature and should embody the above-mentioned four principles.

C. A government should be formed within a fixed time, in accordance with the terms of the Constitution, to take over the administration of Palestine from the mandatory power. . . .

This is the one and only course that the Arabs of Palestine are prepare to take. . . .

The Arabs of Palestine are, therefore, solidly determined to oppose, with all the means at their disposal, any scheme that provides for the dissection, segregation or partition of their tiny country or that gives to a minority, on the ground of creed, special and preferential rights or status.

They will oppose such schemes, in the same zeal and with the same sacrifice that any other people would do under the same circumstances.

Palestine Should Be Partitioned

Abba Hillel Silver

In this 1947 speech to the UN General Assembly's Committee on Palestine, Abba Hillel Silver argues that Palestine should be partitioned and the Jewish people given a home there. He states that Palestine was the home to Jewish people thousands of years before Arab people first conquered it, and a far-reaching Jewish civilization had already been created there. Silver contends that the national home promised by the Balfour Declaration and the Palestine Mandate is the only solution to "the Jewish problem." Abba Hillel Silver was a rabbi and an influential Zionist leader and activist for Jewish statehood and was considered among the most prominent leaders of American Judaism. A spokesperson for the Jewish Agency for Palestine, he participated as a representative of the Jewish Agency at the United Nations General Assembly sessions in 1947–1948.

SOURCE. Abba Hillel Silver, "Palestine Partition Acceptable," *Vital Speeches of the Day*, vol. 14, October 15, 1947, pp. 10–15. Reproduced by permission.

When the Allies liberated Palestine in 1917 along with other parts of the former Ottoman Empire, Palestine was a segment of a Turkish province. There was no politically or culturally distinct or distinguishable Arab nation in that province. There never had been. . . .

By the time the Arabs conquered Palestine in 684 A.D., the Jewish people had already completed nearly 2,000 years of national history in that country, during which time they created a civilization which decidedly influenced the course of mankind, gave rise both to Judaism and Christianity, produced the Bible and brought forth prophets, saints and spiritual leaders who are venerated not only by Judaism, but by Christianity and Islam as well. . . .

The very identity of Palestine as a unit of human society is an achievement of Jewish history. The country lost its separate character with the Jewish dispersion and only assumed a specific role in history when the Palestine mandate was ratified. The mandate acknowledged this history by setting Palestine in a distinct and separate context in relation to the Arab world. "I am persuaded," declared [U.S.] President [Woodrow] Wilson on March 3, 1919, "that the Allied nations with the fullest concurrence of our own Government and people are agreed that in Palestine shall be laid the foundation of a Jewish Commonwealth."

Speaking in the House of Lords on June 27, 1923, Lord Milner, who called himself "a strong supporter of the pro-Arab policy," stated:

"Palestine can never be regarded as a country on the same footing as the other Arab countries. You cannot ignore all history and tradition in the matter . . . and the future of Palestine cannot possibly be left to be determined by the temporary impressions and feelings of the Arab majority in the country in the present day."

When the Palestine mandate therefore recognized "the historical connection of the Jewish people with Palestine" it was only stating a fact that was universally acknowledged through the ages. And when it gave international recognition to the grounds for reconstituting the Jewish national home in that country . . . it was only reaffirming the fact that the Jewish people had never surrendered the hope of national restoration in its ancestral homeland. For to the Jews Palestine was not merely a place of sacred shrines as to Christians and Moslems, but the home of their exiled people, the land of their national destiny, and throughout the dark centuries of persecu-

Rabbi Abba Hillel Silver, the chairman of the Jewish Agency for Palestine, speaks in 1948 during a rally at Madison Square Garden in New York to celebrate the newly established state of Israel. (Leo Rosenthal/ Pix Inc./Time Life Pictures/Getty Images.)

tion and wandering there were continuous efforts to return to it. . . .

The British and Partition

It may be pertinent to recall that the principle of partition on which the majority report of the Committee is based was first projected by the all-British Royal Commission in 1937. At that time the British Government accepted that recommendation in principle and declared:

"In supporting a solution of the Palestine problem by means of partition, His Majesty's Government are much impressed by the advantages which it offers to the Arabs and the Jews. The Arabs would obtain their national independence and thus be enabled to cooperate on an equal footing with the Arabs of neighboring countries in the cause of Arab unity and progress. They would be finally delivered from all fear of Jewish domination. On the other hand, partition would secure the establishment of the Jewish National Home and relieve it from any possibility of its being subjected in the future to Arab rule. It would convert the Jewish National Home into a Jewish State with full control over immigration. Above all, fear and suspicion would be replaced by a sense of confidence and security, and both peoples would obtain, in the words of the Commission, 'the estimable boon of peace.'" . . .

> Palestine offers to [Jews] that which they need most and cannot find anywhere else: the chance of a real home, . . . the insurance of permanency.

In 1947 the British Government proposed another examination of the Palestine problem, this time by the United Nations. . . . This committee has now submitted a report which recommends a plan of partition coupled with economic union. . . .

The Issue of Jewish Displaced Persons

The Jewish Agency . . . wishes to indicate at the outset its full approval of all but one of the eleven unanimous recommendations made by the committee. On the sixth recommendation, of which it does not disapprove, it would like to make this observation. The sixth recommendation calls upon the General Assembly "to undertake immediately the initiation and execution of an international arrangement whereby the problem of the distressed European Jews, of whom approximately 250,000 are in assembly centers, will be dealt with as a matter of extreme urgency for the alleviation of their plight and of the Palestine problem." . . .

> There is but one solution to [the Jewish] problem, a national home.

The report of your Special Committee refers to the "intense urge" of these distressed persons to be allowed to go to Palestine.

The "intense urge" of the Jewish displaced persons to proceed to Palestine and the refusal of most of them to go anywhere else springs not only from their realization that the prospects of their admission to other countries are slight in the extreme, and even then only of a very limited scope. It springs preeminently from the fact that Palestine offers to them that which they need most and cannot find anywhere else: the chance of a real home, the prospect of a life in congenial surroundings, the insurance of permanency.

All the longing of these uprooted people for a life of peace and dignity, for a normal and secure existence finds expression in this "intense urge" to go to Palestine. . . . And if it be countered that mere desire does not create a right, a complete answer is that that desire was the basis for the creation of the right by the Balfour Declaration and the League of Nations mandate.

That desire was recognized as morally so compelling that it led the victorious Allies in the First World War to establish solemn international commitments guaranteeing the legal right of Jews to go to Palestine. . . .

The Jewish Problem in General

The twelfth recommendation of the committee, which was not unanimously opposed by the Committee, reads: "It is recommended that in the appraisal of the Palestine question, it be accepted as incontrovertible that any solution for Palestine cannot be considered as a solution of the Jewish problem in general." We are at a loss to understand the meaning of this recommendation. . . . The "Jewish problem in general" is not a problem of Jewish immigration or of refugees. It is the age-old problem of Jewish national homelessness.

There is but one solution to this problem, a national home. This was the basic Jewish problem which was faced by the Balfour Declaration and the mandate, and to which the proper solution was given—the reconstitution of the national home of the Jewish people in Palestine.

Without attempting at this stage a detailed analysis of the solution recommended by the minority of three members of the Special Committee, we must state at once that we find it wholly unacceptable. . . . This minority report proposes the establishment of an independent Federal State of Palestine, consisting of what are described as an Arab and a Jewish "State," though they are, in fact, little more than semi-autonomous cantons or provinces.

It is obvious that under the constitutional provisions envisaged in this recommendation, Palestine would become in effect an Arab State with two Jewish enclaves, in which the Jews would be frozen in the position of a permanent minority of the population of the Federal State. Under the proposed constitution the Jewish province would not have control over immigration even within the narrow confines of its own borders. Nor would it have control over its own fiscal policies. Not only with regard to the crucial question of immigration, but also with regard to many other matters of fundamental importance, the ultimate power of decision will rest with the Arab majority of the proposed Federal State. . . .

The plan entails for the Jews all the disadvantages of partition—and a very bad partition geographically—without the compensating advantages of a real partition; statehood, independence and free immigration. . . .

Jewish Acceptance of Partition

Partition clearly was never contemplated by the Balfour Declaration of the mandate. It was intended that Palestine, the whole of Palestine, shall ultimately become a Jewish State. This is the clear testimony of Mr. [David] Lloyd George, who was the British Prime Minister at the time of the issuance of the Declaration. The land referred to as Palestine in the Declaration included what is now Trans-Jordan. The Royal Commission of 1937 declared that "the field in which the Jewish national home was to be established was understood at the time of the Balfour Declaration to be the whole of historic Palestine." That area has already been partitioned. . . .

> The Jewish people of Palestine stand ready to assume immediately all responsibilities which the establishment of the Jewish State will involve.

To return to the basic solution of partition proposed by the Special Committee: It entails, as we have said, a very heavy sacrifice on the part of the Jewish people. But if such a sacrifice is made the inexorable condition of an immediate and final solution, we would be prepared to assume the responsibility for recommending acquiescence to the supreme organs of our movement, subject, of course, to further discussion of the constitution and territorial provisions. . . .

We would be prepared to do so because the proposal makes possible the immediate re-establishment of the Jewish State, an ideal for which our people ceaselessly strove through the centuries, and because it ensures immediate and continuing Jewish immigration which, as events have demonstrated is possible only under a Jewish State. We would do so also as our contribution to the solution of a grave international problem and as evidence of our willingness to join with the community of nations in an effort to bring peace at last to the troubled land which is precious to the heart of mankind.

We are impressed with the recommendation in the report of an economic union between the two states. We approve of the conclusion reached by the committee that "in view of the limited area and resources of Palestine, it is essential that, to the extent feasible, and consistent with the creation of two independent states, the economic unity of the country should be preserved."

This appears to us to be a progressive and statesman-like conception of great promsie. The Jewish Agency is prepared to accept this proposal of an economic union. . . .

A Jewish Nation in Palestine

We have builded a nation in Palestine. That nation now demands its independence. It will not be dislodged. Its national status will not be denied. We are asked to make an enormous sacrifice to attain that which, if uninterfered with, we would have attained long ago. In sadness, and most reluctantly, we are prepared to make this sacrifice. Beyond it we cannot, we will not go. . . .

The Jewish people of Palestine stands ready to assume immediately all responsibilities which the establishment of the Jewish State will involve. . . .

Twenty-five years ago a similar international organization recognized the historic claims of the Jewish people, sanctioned our program and set us firmly on the road of realization. We were not then regarded as intruders or invaders, not even by the foremost leaders and spokesmen of the Arab world, but as a people returning home after a long, sad exile. The world approved and acclaimed the return of Israel to its ancient homeland.

United Nations General Assembly Vote on the Partition Plan for Palestine, 1947			
"Yes" to Partition	**"No" to Partition**	**Abstain**	**Absent**
Australia	Afghanistan	Argentina	Thailand
Belgium	Cuba	Chile	
Bolivia	Egypt	China	
Brazil	Greece	Colombia	
Byelorussia	India	El Salvador	
Canada	Iran	Ethiopia	
Costa Rica	Iraq	Honduras	
Czechoslovakia	Lebanon	Mexico	
Denmark	Pakistan	United Kingdom	
Dominican Republic	Saudi Arabia	Yugoslavia	
Ecuador	Syria		
France	Turkey		
Guatemala	Yemen		
Haiti			
Iceland			
Liberia			
Luxembourg			
Netherlands			
New Zealand			
Nicaragua			
Norway			
Panama			
Paraguay			
Peru			
Philippines			
Poland			
Sweden			
Ukraine			
Union of South Africa			
USSR			
USA			
Uruguay			
Venezuela			

Compiled by editor

The statesmen of the world faced the tragic problem of Jewish national homelessness and they set about to solve it.

The Jewish people was confirmed in its right to rebuild its national life in its historic home. It eagerly seized the long hoped-for opportunity and proceeded to rebuild that ancient land of Israel in a manner which evoked the admiration of the whole world. It has made the wilderness blossom as the rose. Surely this great international body, surveying this faithful and fruitful work, will wish to see that work continued, that undertaking advanced, that hope of the centuries consummated. It will be a noble achievement which will redound to the everlasting glory of this world organization. It will be a supreme act of international justice.

Arab States Have No Right to Intervene in Israel

Abba Eban

In the following 1948 speech to the United Nations, Abba Eban calls upon the United Nations (UN) Security Council to instruct the Arab states to end their acts of aggression against the state of Israel. He argues that the acts are unprovoked and a violation of the UN charter and international law. The Arab states have clearly stated that their use of armed force against Israel is political and that their goal is to destroy Israel and make all of Palestine an Arab state. Abba Eban was an Israeli statesman and diplomat. He served Israel in many capacities, including as Israel's first Ambassador to the UN, a member of the Knesset (Israeli Parliament), chief delegate to the UN, minister of education and culture, and foreign minister.

SOURCE. Abba Eban, "The War of Independence," Jewish Media Fund, July 13, 1948.

There is not a single person in this room or outside it who does not know in the depths of his heart that the Arab States, by resuming their attacks upon Israel, have committed an act of aggression within the meaning of Chapter VII of the [UN] Charter. Their armed forces are operating beyond their frontiers for purposes which the Charter specifically forbids. They are using force against the territorial integrity and political independence of the State of Israel in a manner inconsistent with the purposes of the United Nations. Their object, which they openly confess, is to secure the violent extinction of the State of Israel, the establishment of which was recommended by the General Assembly. . . .

It should not be necessary at this stage to provide elaborate evidence in order to prove the aggressive character of these warlike movements upon which the armies of the Arab States have launched themselves—with conspicuous and welcome lack of success. . . .

The principles of the Charter themselves proclaim these operations as acts of aggression. . . . For here we are in the unusual position of not being faced with any conflict of views on the question of who began the fighting. When the first official phase of this aggression began on 15 May, representatives of the Arab States showered documents upon this Council, . . . asserting that they had taken the initiative for using armed force outside their frontiers with the purpose of overthrowing the political independence and territorial integrity of a neighboring State, whose existence they dislike.

> Not one of the conditions which make the use of armed force legitimate under the [UN] Charter exists or has ever been claimed to exist.

Arab States Have Violated International Law

Under the Charter, they are, of course, entitled to dislike the existence of the State of Israel. But under the Charter, they are most emphatically and categorically forbidden to use armed force against the political independence or territorial integrity of that State, or indeed, to use armed force against anybody in Palestinian territory for any purpose whatever "save in the common interest" of the United Nations, or in defense of their own territories, if these territories had been unprovocably attacked. Not one of the conditions which make the use of armed force legitimate under the Charter exists or has ever been claimed to exist in respect of these acts.

At the 302nd meeting of the Security Council the representative of the Arab States read statements . . . , asserting the political ambitions whereby they are animated and the violent means which they use in their support. On that occasion, the representative of the United States said of these declarations:

> Their statements are the best evidence we have of the international character of this aggression . . . They tell us quite frankly that their business in Palestine is political and that they are there to establish a unitary State . . . Therefore . . . we have the highest type of evidence concerning the international violation of the law: namely the admission by those who are committing this violation. . . .

And finally, the representative of the United States, referring to the claim of the Arabs that their operations aimed at the maintenance of peace, said:

> This is equivalent in its absurdity to the legend that these five armies are there to maintain peace, while they are conducting a bloody war. . . .

Concessions to Promote Peace

Cease-fire resolutions were repeatedly sponsored, accepted by the Government of Israel, rejected by the Arab States, re-examined by the Security Council, and eventually served up on 29 May [1948] in the form of a resolution which combined the call for a cease-fire with the satisfaction of what the United Kingdom representative called the "political demands which the Arabs consider reasonable." . . .

As a further inducement to the Arab States to refrain from the use of armed force, encroachments upon the sovereignty of Israel were demanded in that matter wherein its sovereignty is most vital and cherished, the matter of immigration. . . .

Addressing the Security Council five weeks ago, I took leave to enquire whether any State represented around this table would willingly neglect opportunities for improving its defense for a period of four weeks, if it had complete certainty that at the end of those four weeks, the armies of five neighboring States would sweep upon it in converging aggression. We further expressed doubts whether any State represented here would willingly submit its immigration policy, based upon its own right of internal jurisdiction, to the scrutiny or control of anyone else. Yet the State of Israel did accept these restrictive conditions, which it believes should never have been imposed upon it. It allowed its scanty defensive resources to remain unaugmented during the period which it knew to be merely a prelude for further attacks upon its boundaries and its political integrity. It allowed the hand of external control to reach into the rights of immigration, which are the very substance of its national purpose and ideal. It was able to accept these limitations because they were imposed for a specified period of brief duration, and because the Government of Israel, born out of a United Nations judgment and recommendation, has been eager at all times to affirm its fidelity to the principles and the processes of the Charter. . . .

> The Government of Israel . . . has been eager at all times to affirm its fidelity to the principles and the processes of the [UN] Charter.

The Truce Is Dead

On the morning of 9 July the period of the four weeks' truce expired. Owing to the Arab refusal to grant a prolongation, it was not renewed. . . .

At any rate, the truce is dead. The apparatus of observance and supervision has disintegrated. The readiness of the Government of Israel to agree to a four-weeks continuation was most contemptuously rejected on the Arab side, and in the absence either of continuous validity or of mutual acceptance, that Jewish offer also belongs to the history of these recent weeks. In an admirable last-minute effort to keep war at bay while the next stage was contemplated, the Mediator turned to both par-

During his time as Israel's ambassador to the United Nations, Abba Eban (center) confers with his boss, Israeli foreign minister Golda Meir (left), and with Israeli delegation staff member Gideon Rafael (second from left) at a meeting of the UN General Assembly in New York in 1957. (**AP Images.**)

> "What we have to ensure is that the whole tide of invasion is ordered back to the territory from which it arose."

ties and asked them to agree to an unconditional cease-fire for a period of ten days. . . . The Government of Israel accepted this proposal. . . . The Arab Government rejected it. Before the previous truce had even expired, Egyptian forces in the coastal sector of the Negeb [in southern Israel] launched their assault. Their commander was found, on capture, to possess operation orders which show conclusively that his Government had planned not merely to avoid prolongation, but even to launch the aggression anew before the statutory period of the existing truce had expired. . . .

Arab Aggression Must Stop

It is therefore the considered view of the Government of Israel that the only action consonant with the duty of the Security Council at this hour would be to determine an act of Arab aggression, arising out of the Arab decision to resume hostilities and, as a provisional measure under Article 40, to order that aggression immediately and unconditionally to cease. . . .

We need no repetition of a truce with invading armies poised in suspended violence upon Israel's frontiers. We need a deterrent from aggression. We need those invading armies to go home so that the frontiers of Israel become the frontiers of a durable peace. A truce, by its very nature, crystallizes aggression at the point which it has reached at the time the truce comes into operation. It therefore carries with it the seed of possibly renewed war. What we have to ensure is that the whole tide of invasion is ordered back to the territory from which it arose. . . .

It seems well for all parties to this dispute and for all who hope to help bring it to an end, to focus their attention all the time upon the central issue. That issue is the immovable determination of the State of Israel to exist and survive. This State is the product of the most sustained historic tenacity which the ages recall. Somehow this people, in the very climax of its agony, has managed to generate the cohesion, the energy and the confidence to bring the third Jewish commonwealth into existence. . . . The Jewish people has not striven towards this goal for twenty centuries in order that, having once been achieved, with the full endorsement of international opinion, it will now be surrendered in response to an illegitimate and unsuccessful campaign of aggression. Whatever else changes, this will not. . . .

Israel's Immigration Policy Nonnegotiable

The policy of the Government of Israel is to seek relations of harmony with the neighboring Arab States on the basis of its own complete freedom and integrity. It was therefore compelled to reject certain proposals which encroached upon its sovereignty in a way that has seldom been suggested in respect of any independent State. It affirmed, and it now re-affirms, its inability to agree to any encroachment upon or limitation of the free sovereignty of the people of Israel in its independent state. It must be particularly emphatic in its opposition to any infringement of Israel's independence and sovereignty as regards immigration policy. . . .

The Government of Israel made it clear that there could be no question of any Israeli Government accepting the slightest derogation from Israel's sovereignty as regards control of its immigration policy in favor of any joint or international body. . . .

To portray the possibilities of Jewish immigration, drawing from a pathetically depleted reservoir of Jewish remnants left alive in the world, to portray this State of Israel approaching its first million of population as a potential threat to the far-flung Arab Empire, with its 40

> "It is for the [UN] Security Council, therefore, to 'forbid armed force in the settlement of this problem.'"

millions of population, is to accept uncritically one of the most unfounded of Arab contentions. . . .

We cannot accept that "Jewish immigration into the Jewish area of Palestine concerns . . . the neighboring Arab world." We declare that immigration into Israel is the business of Israel alone. The Governments of Egypt, Transjordan and Syria have no more jurisdiction in this question than has the Government of Israel in any of their internal affairs. The suggestion that a neighboring State might exercise a power of challenge or veto against Israel's immigration policy is to us as fantastic as it would be to suggest that Canada should be able to influence the immigration policy of the United States on the grounds of geographical proximity and a mutual continental interest. . . .

A Right to Political Sovereignty

The insistence by the State of Israel upon its unrestricted sovereignty is by no means incompatible with its vision of Arab-Jewish co-operation. Indeed the doctrine of sovereign equality which is the basis of the Charter makes political independence the essential condition of regional co-operation in the modern world. When we speak of an independent sovereign Israel joining with its neighbors in projects of regional development, we set no precedent. We depart from no principle which is based upon the Charter and commonly accepted as the most advanced political ideal of the contemporary world. . . . The Arab League itself, little as it might have done in the sphere of social and economic progress on a regional basis, at least has the merit of respecting the sovereignty of its individual members. Even two countries so akin as Syria and Lebanon, joined together by common economic interests in so many enterprises, cannot envisage their co-operation except on the basis of the free unrestricted political sovereignty of each one. How far-fetched then it is to imagine that this principle of political independence which cannot be compromised even between peoples of similar social and cultural background, can be obscured in the relations of Israel with its neighbors. . . .

Only when aggression dies down, only when armed force is forbidden in the settlement of this problem, only when it is made "prohibitively unprofitable" for the Arab States to employ it, only then does the prospect of any peaceful relations emerge upon the horizon, beckoning the initiative and foresight of both parties. We should be wrong to spend time considering a final peace unless we were sure that these obstacles could be surmounted. It is for the Security Council, therefore, to "forbid armed force in the settlement of this problem."

Outside Factors Contributed to the Birth of Israel

Geoffrey Wheatcroft

In the following viewpoint, Geoffrey Wheatcroft contends that while Jewish heroism, sacrifice, diplomacy, military discipline, and terrorism helped bring about the birth of the state of Israel, they were not the only contributing factors. Without world events over which the Zionists had no control the state would not have been born. World War I and World War II, as well as the positions and actions of the British, the Americans, and the Soviets, all had a part. Adolf Hitler was a major factor. Wheatcroft asserts that without Hitler, "Israel could not have been born when and as it was." Geoffrey Wheatcroft is a British journalist and author.

SOURCE. Geoffrey Wheatcroft, *The Controversy of Zion: Jewish Nationalism, the Jewish State, and the Unresolved Jewish Dilemma.* Boston, MA: Addison-Wesley, 1996. Copyright © 1996. Reprinted by permission of Basic Books, a member of Perseus Books Group.

On 14 May 1948, a new state was born. The Zionist General Council proclaimed . . . that 'foreign rule' would no longer be tolerated in the country. In Washington, the [Harry S.] Truman administration immediately extended *de facto* [unofficial] recognition to the new state of Israel, and three days later Soviet Russia capped this with *de jure* [according to law] recognition. . . .

As independence dawned, [first Prime Minister of Israel David] Ben-Gurion echoed an old Zionist slogan: 'Like other nations, it is the right of the Jewish people to determine its history under its own sovereignty.' This seemed to be the central moral accomplishment, but the rhetoric obscured the reality. On the face of it the Jews had at last, for the first time in nearly two thousand years, taken their destiny in their own hands and were shaping their own history. The creation of Israel, with its subsequent history, was indeed a breath-taking achievement, a triumph of will and human spirit, won, as that one-time Zionist enthusiast Winston Churchill could have said, by blood, toil, tears, and sweat, by heroic battles against the odds.

> The new state would not have been born without factors which the Zionists did not control.

Contributing Factors to the Birth of Israel

But it was not that alone. Although the new Israeli people wanted to make their own story, it was in truth still to a large degree being made for them from outside. For all the heroism and sacrifice of the pioneers, for all [first Israeli president Chaim] Weizmann's long and patient diplomacy, for all the military discipline of the Haganah [Jewish defense organization] and for all the frank terror of the Sternists [terrorist group] and Irgun [militant Zionist group] the new state would not have been born without factors which the Zionists did not control. One great war had led to the establishment of a Jewish homeland, another to a new conjunction in international affairs. Israel was born when the British were too worn out by war to continue their own imperial burden, when the American administration had decided to back the new state, despite many misgivings in the State Department and even in the White House, when Soviet Russia, for even more irrelevant and cynical reasons, decided that it too would act as a sponsor.

Above all, it was born after the greatest catastrophe in Jewish history. More than thirty years later, [author] George Steiner wrote a strange fantasy, in which [Nazi dictator Adolf] Hitler is found in Latin America where, not having died at all, he had fled like [Nazi SS officer Adolf] Eichmann. At one moment 'AH' muses about the fate of Germany and the Jews: 'And the Reich begat Israel.' To some Israelis this literary conceit seemed distasteful, and to some rigorous Zionists it was a point of principle that the Zionist vision was in no way affected or further justified by the fate of the European Jews. This flew in the face of common sense. Hitler was the most unsuccessful politician of all time, for all his vast and insane deeds: he left Germany divided for nearly half a century, left Europe as far west as the Elbe in the hands of his mortal enemies the Bolsheviks, and left his even more hated enemies, the Jews, with a voice in world affairs for the first time. But for him, Israel could not have been born when and as it was.

> It was wholly original, an 'idea in history' made flesh.

Why Israel Was Unique

As for Ben-Gurion's other phrase, the old Zionist aspiration, that too was implausible. 'Like other nations' was quite obviously just what Israel was not. It was like no other country on earth, and in many ways did not pretend to be. This was no England or France, no United States or Soviet Russia, not even another Romania or Serbia, the pattern against which [Russian author Leo] Tolstoy had warned the early Zionists. It was wholly original, an 'idea in history' made flesh. And, if its relationship with the outside world was different, its relationship with the Jewish Dispersion was also different from that of other new-born countries with their own Diasporas [dispersions], a difference of kind rather than degree.

One uniquely distinctive feature which made the new state unlike other nations was its Magna Carta or Bill of Rights, the Law of Return which gave any Jew anywhere on earth (begging the question of who was a Jew) the right to settle in Israel. It was no abstract notion. In the first years from 1948 to 1951 there was a huge immigration, more than 650,000. They came as survivors from Europe, notably from Romania where a larger proportion of the Jewish population than in most east European countries had survived the Germans. They came in increasing numbers from the Arab countries, from Morocco far to the west of Israel, from Irak [Iraq] to the east, from Yemen to the south. This

> Most Jews were happy that Israel had happened, and happy to leave it at that.

was something few had foreseen. . . . The creation of the Jewish state sent convulsions through the Arab world. In 1949, Israel signed armistices with the neighbouring countries which still did not officially recognise her, Egypt, Jordan, Syria, Lebanon. Humiliating defeat led in turn to a surge of populist nationalism in those countries, which threatened the old regime: the king of Jordan was assassinated in 1951, the stamp-collecting King Farouk of Egypt was deposed the next year. Under old or new leaders, these countries talked about crushing the Zionist interloper, but only talked. The fledgeling state profited from its neighbours: from their verbal violence, from their appearance of strength if only numerically, and from their actual military incompetence. It was not only

British police load their equipment onto trucks in December 1947. Their departure represented the first step in Britain's evacuation of its personnel from Palestine. (**AP Images.**)

that the Israelis could say, as the anti-imperialist (and antisemitic) [writer Hilaire] Belloc had said, 'Whatever happens, we have got The Maxim gun and they have not.' Along with their great advantage in technology and weaponry, the Israelis had the crucial advantage of morale, of believing that they were fighting for something very precious, not to say for their very existence. . . .

The Jewish Reaction to the New State

The creation of the new state and its embattled survival were the cause of intense pride to Jews everywhere. . . .

Most Jews were happy that Israel had happened, and happy to leave it at that. They did not have the time or inclination to examine what the creation of a Jewish state had done to the Jewish Question. . . .

The Jewish state had been created. Jewish opposition to Zionism, which had had such a long history, and often a morally and intellectually honourable one, was almost extinguished. It became morally intolerable for any Jew to oppose Israel, or even publicly to criticise her. At the same time, only a small minority of Jews actively wished to live in this Jewish state. Most of the Israeli population was composed of people, or the descendants of people, who had gone there because they had no choice: of refugees fleeing Polish antisemitism and Hitler's mad persecution between the wars, of the remnant of mass murder after 1945 who were offered refuge nowhere else, of the Jews of Araby who were now driven out of their native lands and likewise had nowhere else to go.

The Connection Between the Holocaust and the Creation of Israel

Evyatar Friesel

In the following viewpoint, Evyatar Friesel argues that the Holocaust was a factor in, but was not the basis for, the 1948 establishment of the state of Israel. Jewish statehood was the ultimate goal of the Zionists but not the impetus for the member nations of the United Nations to vote for the partition of Palestine and creation of a Jewish state. During their discussions, the member nations did not attach much significance to the Holocaust; their primary concerns were the practical problem of the Jewish refugees and the possibility that the Palestinian problem might escalate into war. Evyatar Friesel is a historian and an internationally recognized author. He served as

SOURCE. Evyatar Friesel, *Major Changes within the Jewish People in the Wake of the Holocaust: Proceedings of the Ninth Yad Vashem International Historical Conference.* Jerusalem, Israel: Yad Va-shem, 1996. Copyright © Yad Vashem Publications. Reproduced by permission of Yad Vashem Publications.

state archivist of Israel from 1993 to 2001 and later an emeritus professor at Hebrew University in Jerusalem. The following viewpoint is from an abridged version of the original article.

It is widely believed that the catastrophe of European Jewry during World War II had a decisive influence on the establishment of the Jewish state in 1948. According to this thesis, for the Jews the Holocaust triggered a supreme effort toward statehood, based on the understanding that only a Jewish state might again avoid the horrors of the 1940s. For the nations of the world, shocked by the horror of the extermination and burdened by feelings of guilt, the Holocaust convinced them that the Jews were entitled to a state of their own. All these assumptions seem extremely doubtful. . . .

The quest for a Jewish state had always been paramount in Zionist thought and action. For tactical reasons official Zionism was cautious in explaining its ultimate aims, especially when addressing general public opinion. Terms other than "state" were used in various political documents or official utterances by leading Zionist statesmen: Jewish home, Jewish National Home, commonwealth, Jewish commonwealth. But there is no reason to doubt that the ultimate aim of the Zionist mainstream was the creation of a state in Palestine. . . .

On May 15, 1948, the State of Israel was proclaimed. A new political reality was thus established. In the words of the Israeli diplomat Walter Eytan: If this Jewish state came into being . . . it was not primarily because the United Nations had recommended it. . . . When the day of independence dawned, the decision was Israel's alone.

> Regarding the deliberations of the United Nations and its bodies in 1947–1948, it is difficult to find evidence that the Holocaust played a decisive or even significant role [in establishing a Jewish state].

The Holocaust's Role in the UN Decision

Was there, then, a connection between the Holocaust and the creation of Israel? Is it conceivable that the two most decisive events in modern Jewish history could occur almost simultaneously and not be linked? Is it possible that the emergence of the Jewish state was unrelated to the terrible disaster of the Jewish people and to the remorse of the nations of the world?

Regarding the deliberations of the United Nations and its bodies in 1947–1948, it is difficult to find evidence that the Holocaust played a decisive or even significant role. No bloc of nations proclaimed during the UN discussions on Palestine that its foremost aim was the creation of a Jewish state. (On the other hand, an important group of countries did favor the transformation of Palestine into an Arab state.) What impelled the international body was the practical problem of the Jewish refugees and, even more, the awareness that the Palestinian problem was drifting toward chaos and war.

The actual General Assembly decision regarding partition was made possible by the support of the two super-powers. However, although their agreement was a necessary condition for the UN partition resolution, it was not in itself sufficient. The majority of the UN members who voted for the resolution deserve additional consideration, especially since the American representatives abstained from lobbying too actively for the UNSCOP [United Nations Special Committee on Palestine] proposal. True, some of the countries of the Western bloc did display an understanding—and, in a few cases, even a genuine interest—in Jewish and Zionist aspirations, but, for most of the states represented at the UN, the Jewish problem was something far removed from their concerns. It was, however, natural and understandable for them to go along with the Soviet-American proposition, given the great political and moral weight of such an agreement between the super-powers. And since the measure of agreement between the United States and the Soviet Union neutralized clear-cut international rivalries, their tendency was to consider the Palestine question in terms of political realities. Factors such as the historical connection of the Jewish people to Palestine, or feelings of remorse because of the recent Jewish tragedy were hardly heard, if at all. Indeed, were they to be expected? It is only reasonable to assume that the great majority of UN members considered the Palestine question in "practical" terms. That attitude was well expressed in Article XII of the UNSCOP principles, which stressed that there could be no connection between the Palestinian issue and the Jewish problem.

> It seems clear that both the Holocaust and Jewish statehood had some common historical foundations.

Consequently, when at the beginning of 1948, it became increasingly clear that partition was not going to prevent a war in Palestine, the UN . . . started looking for a different, "practical" solution. All of which only emphasizes how modest a role the facts about and the reactions to the Holocaust played in the considerations of the international community. Even if there were a similarity in the actual outcome under consideration, there was little in common between the reasons impelling Jews and Zionists toward Jewish statehood and the reasoning behind the United Nations resolution for the partition of Palestine.

The Connection from the Jewish Viewpoint

Obviously, from the standpoint of Jewish history, there is a different perspective about the relationship between Jewish statehood and the Holocaust. One factor to be pondered is the subjective attitudes of post-Holocaust Jewry regarding the Holocaust. The process of weaving the knowledge of the Holocaust into the texture of Jewish historical consciousness, which began with the extermination and which has continued ever since, has a sense of its own. It is an ongoing labor in which diverse segments of the Jewish people . . . tend to emphasize different aspects of the tragedy that befell the Jewish people during World War II. The nearness in time between the Holocaust and the birth of Israel also encourages the connection between the events, if only for the purpose of self-consolation. But their enormous historical significance demands sharp and unpitying lucidity in order to understand their place in the history of the Jewish people. The complex logic of this historical problem suggests apparently contradictory conclusions: that there was a relationship between the Holocaust and the emergence of Israel—and that there was none.

> A distinction should be made between the influence of the Holocaust as a historical occurrence . . . and the Holocaust as a molding factor in later Jewish consciousness.

Either way, it seems clear that both the Holocaust and Jewish statehood had some common historical foundations. Each expressed, in its own way, the final crisis of the relationship between Jewish and non-Jewish society, a relationship based on patterns of co-existence that had developed in Europe since the Middle Ages. In that sense, both represented radical responses. Rather than converging, however, both responses ran parallel and in opposite directions. Considered alongside the establishment of the Jewish state, the Holocaust represented the *sitra ahra*, the other face, of Jewish existence—the side of darkness and destruction, against the side of creation and continuity. The reaction to the Holocaust brought about a peculiar tension in Jewish life, a sense of *aharit ha-yamim* ("end of days"), reminiscent of the response to the earlier disasters in Jewish history, such as the destruction of the First and the Second Temples [in Jerusalem], or the expulsion of the Jews from Spain in the late Middle Ages. This consciousness brought about an awakening of inner strength, blending despair and grim hope that permeated the political struggle of the Jews to prevail in Palestine and to overcome all obstacles in spite of and against all odds. This spirit, uncharacteristic—and perhaps undesirable—in times when the life of a people runs its normal course, was an essential component of the Zionist and Jewish effort to establish their state in Palestine. Any examination of what happened in the late 1940s in Palestine and at the United Nations shows that the Jews were not the strongest among the political participants in that international drama. But they were possessed by a singleness of purpose and by a sense of total dedication to a constructive goal that were unmatched by any of the other direct or indirect participants in the question of Palestine.

The Holocaust as a Molding Factor

That characteristic in Jewish political activism became a powerful lever in a situation that, for reasons unrelated, had already reached the point of maturation. As we have shown above, in a narrower sense it was the British policy in Palestine, or, more specifically, the White Paper of 1939, that set in motion the process leading toward the political aim of Zionism—the creation of a Jewish state. In the background there were additional long-term factors. The wheels moving toward the emergence of Israel the state reflected developments going back a century at least: the modernization of Jewish society, the rise of Jewish nationalism, the crisis of the Jewish-Gentile relationship in modern times, and the emergence of Zionism itself. The extermination of European Jewry happened long after these long or short term forces in Jewish history, striving toward

> The destruction of European Jewry almost rendered the birth of Israel impossible.

national sovereignty and independent statehood, had been set into motion.

True, a distinction should be made between the influence of the Holocaust as a historical occurrence (as we have just done), and the Holocaust as a molding factor in later Jewish consciousness. In the second case there seems little reason to believe that the Holocaust influenced the creation of the Jewish state. In terms of subjective insight, it would take a long time for the Holocaust to be absorbed by the Jewish people in its deeper historical and meta-historical significances. The incorporation of the Holocaust into the collective awareness of the Jewish people is a process that is far from complete. . . . It will take a long time for the Jewish people to learn how to live with the knowledge of the Holocaust and how to merge this knowledge into the complex structure of its millennial historical consciousness, with its varied patterns of shadows and light, tragedy and creation, death and life. The emergence of the State of Israel in 1948 occurred long before then.

A Reverse Point of Contact

Nevertheless, there was a point of contact and influence between the Holocaust and the creation of the Jewish state. It was, however, exactly the reverse of what is commonly assumed: the destruction of European Jewry almost rendered the birth of Israel impossible.

Zionism as an idea and a movement expressed yearnings and needs of very diverse strata of the Jewish people, from the fringe of the almost assimilated to the opposite fringe of those almost untouched by modern secular culture. In its focal point, its vital and most creative mainstream, Zionism was the movement of a broad part of Jewish society, combining a significant degree of cultural integration in the secular world with a high degree of Jewish consciousness. Zionism arose out of a long experience of relations between Jews and non-Jews, where all

the options of mutual understanding had been tried and had failed, up to the point in modern times where only negative solutions remained open—from the Jewish as well as from the non-Jewish perspectives. In this respect Zionism was essentially a product of European Jewry, especially East European Jewry.

Ironically, that sector of the Jewish people was almost completely annihilated in the Holocaust. When the dust settled after the tempest of World War II, and Jewry

At the end of World War II the bodies of murdered victims, most of them Jewish people or political prisoners, are piled on a cart at the German concentration camp Buchenwald in April 1945. (AP Images.)

took stock of its situation, what remained were three major groups of Jews. First, the Jewish communities in Arab lands, soon to be swept by the messianic hope of Israel-reborn, but strangers to the European-grounded social and ideological premises that had created modern Zionism. Second, there were the new Western communities, such as American Jewry, rich and active, but still young and unsettled sociologically and trying to define its status in its new general environment. But the patterns of Jewish life there were developing significantly different from the conditions that had brought about the development of Zionism in Europe. Finally, there was the Jewish community in Palestine—the last creation of a Jewry that was no more.

The most vital segment of modern Jewry, the most settled and vigorous among the Jewish communities, the East European Jewry that had created the Jewish National Home in Palestine and would have been the most able and most prepared to complete the task, had been exterminated in the war. The child of its hopes and endeavors, Israel-the-state, was reborn beside the graves of its fathers and mothers at the Jewish people's darkest hour. Israel came forth smaller and poorer, in the physical and spiritual sense, than she would have had the huge reservoir of manpower and talent within European Jewry attended her birth and kept watch over her cradle. In her internal structure, in her spiritual life, even in her relationship with her surroundings and in her position among the nations of the world, both as a state and as a people, Israel is still enduring the consequences of the Holocaust.

Establishment of the State of Israel Was an Injustice to the Palestinians

Avi Shlaim

In the following viewpoint, Avi Shlaim argues that the Palestinians suffered a great injustice with the establishment of the state of Israel. Israel owes Palestine a debt, which it must repay, he contends. It should not have come as a surprise that Palestinians would not voluntarily give up their right to hold on to their heritage. Shlaim maintains that Arab–Israeli conflict will continue to plague the area until the Israelis stop taking over Palestinian land and agree to an independent Palestinian state. Avi Shlaim is a professor of international relations at Oxford University and a fellow of the British Academy. A frequent contributor to magazines and newspapers and a commentator on radio and television on Middle Eastern affairs, he has authored many books, including *The Iron Wall: Israel and the Arab World*.

SOURCE. Avi Shlaim, "A Somber Anniversary," *The Nation*, vol. 286, May 26, 2008, pp. 11–16. Copyright © 2008 by The Nation Magazine/The Nation Company, Inc. Reproduced by permission.

Israelis approach the sixtieth anniversary of the establishment of their state in a subdued and somber mood. Israeli society is deeply divided, and there is no consensus on how to mark the milestone. On the one hand, Israel can boast some stunning successes: a democratic polity with universal suffrage; a highly developed, some might say overdeveloped, multiparty system; an independent judiciary; a vibrant cultural scene; progressive educational and health services; a high standard of living; and a per capita GDP [gross domestic product] almost the size of Britain's.

The ingathering of the exiles has worked. Israel's population has reached 7,241,000, nearly ten times what it was in 1948. Forty-one percent of the world's Jews live in the Jewish state, speaking the Hebrew language that was confined to liturgy when Zionism was born at the end of the nineteenth century. In its central aim of providing the scattered Jews with a haven, instilling in them a sense of nationhood and forging a modern nation-state, Zionism has been a brilliant success. And these achievements are all the more remarkable against the background of appalling tragedy: the extermination of 6 million Jews by the Nazis during World War II.

> There is no denying that the establishment of the State of Israel involved a massive injustice to the Palestinians.

On the other hand, some failures can be noted. The most pronounced one has been the failure to resolve the conflict with the Arabs, which has accompanied the Zionist enterprise from the very beginning. That conflict involved neighboring Arab states, but in origin and in essence it was a clash between two movements for national liberation: the Jewish one and the Palestinian one. In 1948 the Zionist movement realized its aim of Jewish national self-determination in Palestine. Israel's War of Independence was the Palestinians' catastrophe, *al-Nakba* in Arabic.

The Right to National Self-Determination

The moral case for the establishment of an independent Jewish state was strong, especially in the aftermath of the Holocaust. The case for a Jewish state was also bolstered by the international norm of self-determination for national groups. Based on this norm, the UN partition resolution of November 29, 1947, provided a charter of international legitimacy for the creation of a Jewish state in Palestine. However, there is no denying that the establishment of the State of Israel involved a massive injustice to the Palestinians. Sixty years on, Israel still has not arrived at a reckoning of its sins against the Palestinians, a recognition that it owes the Palestinians a debt that must at some point be repaid.

The conflict with the Palestinians, and with the Arab world at large, has cast a very long shadow over Israel's life. For the first forty-five years of the state's existence, Israel's leaders were unwilling to discuss the right of the Palestinians to national self-determination. . . . The dilemma, in a nutshell, was that the Jewish aspiration to sovereignty in Palestine could not be reconciled with the Palestinian people's natural right to sovereignty over the same country. . . .

The Iron Wall

Ze'ev Jabotinsky, founder of the right-wing Revisionist Zionist movement and spiritual father of the Likud Party, was the first major Zionist leader to acknowledge that the Palestinians were a nation and that they could not be expected to renounce voluntarily their right to hold on to their patrimony. It was, he argued in two seminal articles in 1923, therefore pointless at that early stage in the Zionist enterprise to hold a dialogue

> After knocking their heads in vain against the ramparts, the Palestinians would eventually recognize that they were in a position of permanent weakness.

with the Palestinians; the Zionist program could only be executed unilaterally and by force. Jabotinsky's prescription was to build the Zionist enterprise behind an "iron wall" that the local Arab population would not be able to break. Yet Jabotinsky was not opposed to talking with the Palestinians at a later stage. On the contrary, he believed that after knocking their heads in vain against the ramparts, the Palestinians would eventually recognize that they were in a position of permanent weakness; that would be the time to enter into negotiations with them about their status and national rights in Palestine.

In a way, this is what happened. The history of the State of Israel is a vindication of Jabotinsky's strategy of the iron wall. The Arabs—first the Egyptians, then the Palestinians and then the Jordanians—recognized Israel's invincibility and were compelled to negotiate with it from a position of palpable weakness. The real danger posed by the strategy of the iron wall was that Israeli leaders less sophisticated than Jabotinsky would fall in love with a particular phase of it and refuse to negotiate even when there was someone to talk to on the other side. . . .

The Oslo Accord

The first serious attempt to transcend the iron wall was made by Yitzhak Rabin following the Labor Party's victory at the polls in June 1992. . . . During his first term as prime minister, in the 1970s, Rabin remained implacably opposed to any negotiations with the PLO [Palestine Liberation Organization].

But during his second term, after exhausting all alternatives, Rabin grasped the nettle, which meant negotiating with the PLO. The upshot was the Oslo Accord. . . . What the accord amounted to was PLO recognition of Israel's right to exist, Israeli recognition of the PLO as the representative of the Palestinian people and an understanding between the two sides that the remaining differences between them would be settled by peaceful means.

Water Flows Through Arab–Israeli Disputes

After the 1967 Arab-Israel War, new issues complicated an already complex situation, since Israel took and occupied Jerusalem and the West Bank of the Jordan [River]. Discovering the existence of the huge aquifer under the spine of the mountains of the West Bank, Israel began to pump winter floodwaters into the aquifer to use it as a better water storage area than the Sea of Galilee. Israel refuses to allow the Palestinians in the West Bank to drill deeply for new wells lest they tap this vital storage area. By taking the Golan Heights from Syria, Israel also gained complete control over the Galilee, the upper Jordan River, and even part of the Yarmuk River. This gave Israel effective control over the Jordan River, preventing water diversion downstream by either Jordanians or Palestinians. Indeed, securing control over the water supply was one of several Israeli motivations in launching the 1967 war in the first place.

Throughout the 1970s, 1980s, and 1990s, Israel continued to build settlements in the West Bank, diverting surface water from the Jordan and more groundwater from underground aquifers, in each case lessening the amount of water available for Palestinian towns and cities. The 1973 Arab-Israeli War did nothing to change this situation, nor did the wars of the 1980s in Lebanon and in the Persian Gulf. . . .

In the West Bank, Israeli reoccupation, the Palestinian uprising, and the collapse of much of the regional peace process have at least delayed any hope of more equitable access to surface or groundwater supplies. Hence the water situation for the Palestinian Authority remains dire and will be a vital point of negotiation with Israel.

Hydropolitics are vitally important to Israel, Jordan, Syria, and the Palestinian Authority as they approach the point when they will be using all their available water and yet have rapidly growing populations. Unless there is a major technological breakthrough, and unless greater levels of cooperation can be arranged between these riparian [riverbank-dwelling] peoples, hydropolitics may precipitate ecological disaster and possibly the next war.

SOURCE. *Sara Reguer, "Jordan River,"* Encyclopedia of the Modern Middle East and North Africa, *Philip Mattar, ed., 2nd ed. Detroit: Macmillan Reference USA, 2004.*

The Oslo Accord was a major breakthrough in the century-old conflict between Jews and Arabs in Palestine. It was the first-ever agreement between the two principal parties to the conflict. . . . By signing the agreement, the

> It was simply not reasonable to expect the Palestinians to go forward toward a peace deal when Israel was expropriating more and more of their land.

Palestinians conceded the legitimacy of the Jewish state over 78 percent of what had been the British Mandate of Palestine. What they expected to get in return—though this was not written down in the agreement—was independence over the remaining 22 percent: the West Bank, the Gaza Strip and East Jerusalem.

To be sure, the agreement . . . fell a long way short of the Palestinian aspiration to full independence and statehood. But the agreement did set in motion a gradual and controlled Israeli withdrawal from the occupied Palestinian territories. In the two years following the signing of the accord, substantial progress was achieved. Cooperation between the security services of the two sides was very close, and also progress was made in empowering the Palestinians to govern themselves, culminating in the Oslo II Accord of September 1995. This period wasn't without tensions. . . . But it was the overall success, not the failure, of the Oslo peace process that provoked a right-wing backlash in Israel and the assassination of Rabin by a Jewish religious fanatic in November 1995. . . .

A Step Backward

With the murder of Rabin, the peace process began to falter. In a long-term historical perspective, however, the series of agreements between 1993 and 1999 under the auspices of Oslo were not a failure. Nor were they doomed to fail from the start. They did not collapse under the weight of their own contradictions, as critics like to argue. Rather, the peace process failed because Israel, under the leadership of the Likud, reneged on its side of the original deal.

Likud Prime Minister Benjamin Netanyahu was no friend of the Oslo Accord. He regarded it as incompatible with the historic right of the Jewish people to the entire Land of Israel and with Israel's right to security. Netanyahu spent his three years in power, from 1996 to 1999, in a largely successful attempt to arrest and subvert the peace process. By subverting it, he inflicted serious damage not only on the Palestinians but on his own country and on the Middle East as a whole.

As far back as 1988, the Palestinians had made their choice. They offered Israel recognition and peace in return for a minimal restitution of what had been taken away from them by force. Since then the ball has been in Israel's court. Israel had to choose. Netanyahu and his colleagues in the ultranationalist camp chose to go back on the historic compromise struck by their Labor predecessors and to return to confrontation.

Path to a Full-Scale Uprising

In May 1999 the Israeli electorate deposed Netanyahu and replaced him with Ehud Barak in order to give peace a chance. . . . The most fundamental obstacle to peace with the Palestinians was settlement expansion on the West Bank. . . . This did not violate the letter of the accord, but it most definitely violated the spirit. It was simply not reasonable to expect the Palestinians to go forward toward a peace deal when Israel was expropriating more and more of their land. Land-grabbing and peacemaking do not go well together. This became clear at the Camp David summit in July 2000. The package offered by Barak was not enough to persuade the Palestinian negotiators to give him what he wanted: a formal and final end to the conflict. Following the collapse of the summit, Barak propagated the notion that there was no Palestinian partner for peace. This was not true; there was a Palestinian partner, but not on Barak's terms.

With the collapse of the Camp David summit, the countdown to the outbreak of the next round of violence

> The occupation has to end, not simply because the Palestinians deserve no less but in order to preserve the values for which the State of Israel was created.

began. Ariel Sharon, the leader of the opposition, provided the spark that set off the explosion. On September 28, 2000, flanked by a thousand security men and in deliberate disregard of the sensitivity of Muslim worshipers, Sharon ostentatiously walked into Jerusalem's Haram al-Sharif, the Noble Sanctuary [an Islamic holy place]. His walk-about sparked riots that spread to other Arab areas of East Jerusalem and to other cities. Within a very short time, the riots snowballed into a full-scale uprising—the Al-Aqsa Intifada. The escalating violence, and the belief that there was no Palestinian partner for peace, paved the way to Barak's political demise and to Sharon's Likud victory in the February 2001 election.

Israel's One-Sided Approach

The rise to power of Sharon, the champion of violent solutions, marked the end of any serious negotiations between Israel and the Palestinians. . . . His policy toward the Palestinians consisted of the iron fist inside the iron glove. Under Sharon's leadership Israel reverted to unilateralism in its purest and most unrestrained form. His objective was to set aside the Oslo Accords, to fragment and mutilate the Palestinian territories, to reassert total Israeli control over the West Bank and to deny the Palestinians any independent political existence in Palestine. His long-term aim was to redraw the borders of Greater Israel. . . .

The Israeli right thus provided both the paradigm for solving the conflict with the Palestinians and the politicians who are unable or unwilling to act on it. Consequently, on its sixtieth anniversary, Israel still faces the same dilemma it was faced with forty-one years ago, after seizing new territory in the 1967 war: it can have land or it can have peace. It cannot have both.

The Need for a Two-State Solution

During the past forty-one years Israel has tried every conceivable method of ending the conflict with the Palestinians except the obvious one: ending the occupation. The occupation has to end, not simply because the Palestinians deserve no less but in order to preserve the values for which the State of Israel was created. In any case, whether Israelis like it or not, an independent Palestinian state is inevitable in the long run. . . .

To its credit, the Israeli public has never been as implacably opposed to an independent Palestinian state as the politicians of the right. The question now is whether Israel will give the Palestinians a chance to build that state or strive endlessly to frustrate it. . . . At the time of writing there is precious little evidence to suggest that Israel's leaders are willing to rise to the challenge. They appear united in their determination to preserve Israel's

As a Palestinian woman yells during a protest at the Israeli border near the village of Marwahin, Lebanon, she holds aloft a symbolic key bearing Arabic writing that reads, "We are returning." (**AP Images.**)

military and economic control over the West Bank. Yet there is some ground for optimism. The Palestinians learned from their own mistakes: they put rejection-ism behind them, moderated their program and opted for a two-state solution. It is not beyond the bounds of possibility that the Israelis will one day learn from their mistakes and elect leaders who recognize the need for a genuine two-state solution. Nations, like individuals, are capable of acting rationally—after they have exhausted all the alternatives.

The Balfour Declaration Is Responsible for Instability in the Middle East

Peter Mansfield

In the following viewpoint, Peter Mansfield argues in 1967 that the wording and intent of the 1917 Balfour Declaration was ambiguous and contradicted other British pledges regarding Palestine. He maintains that in retrospect it is believed that the opponents of the declaration lost out because their arguments, although valid, were not strong enough to counter such influences as the Protestant belief in the return of the Jewish people to Zion and British imperialist goals. Because the policy set down by the Balfour Declaration could not be brought into line with other Allied declarations and pledges, there is chronic instability in the Middle East as the Arab population and the Jewish people continue to dispute each other's claims regarding the right to existence of the state of Israel. Peter Mansfield was a British

SOURCE. Peter Mansfield, "Did We Double-cross the Arabs?" *New Statesman*, November 3, 1967. Copyright © 1967 New Statesman, Ltd. Reproduced by permission.

historian, writer, journalist, and commentator who specialized in the contemporary affairs and history of the Middle East.

The root cause of the chronic instability of the Middle East is an irresponsible act of statesmanship of half a century ago. When the Balfour Declaration was issued on 2 November 1917, in the form of a letter from the British Foreign Secretary to Lord Rothschild, saying that His Majesty's Government 'view with favour the establishment in Palestine of a national home for the Jewish people', some members of the [prime minister David] Lloyd George government forecast the storms ahead. [war cabinet member George] Curzon, who had studied Zionist literature, said he 'could not share the optimistic views held concerning the future of Palestine' and he feared that the Declaration 'raised false expectations which could never be realised'. Edwin Montagu, Secretary of State for India and the only Jew in the Cabinet, regarded the Declaration as an anti-Semitic act because it would jeopardise the position of Jews throughout the world. He also believed that it broke promises made to the Arabs and violated the principle of self-determination. These opponents were easily overwhelmed by the confidence of the Declaration's three champions—[Arthur] Balfour, [undersecretary of state Lord Robert] Cecil and Lloyd George himself.

Underlying Motives

Their motives have been the subject of endless speculation. They seem to have been a peculiarly British blend of hard-headed realism and romantic idealism, strongly tinged with hypocrisy. The Declaration's sponsors were so vague about their reasons that they were driven to post hoc rationalisation in

> Had [the British] considered the reactions of . . . the Arabs who formed more than 90 per cent of the population?

later years. Lloyd George told the House of Commons in 1936 that in 1917 the war was going so badly for the Allies that 'we came to the conclusion that it was vital that we should have the sympathies of the Jewish community'. But there is no evidence that they thought of this at the time.

An important influence on the minds of the government was the Bible-reading Protestant belief in the return of the Jews to Zion on which men like Lloyd George (and the agnostic [Winston] Churchill—another enthusiastic Zionist) had been nourished. Imperialist motives also played their part, but it was less the specific aims of balancing French influence in Syria with a pro-British community in Palestine which would also help to protect the Suez Canal (although this was in the back of their minds) than the general idea that the Jews, as civilised Europeans, would carry the white man's burden in an area where Britons were unlikely to do so themselves.

An Independent Jewish National State

Did they understand the implications of their action? Were they aware that the Zionist aim was to make Palestine a Jewish national state? Had they considered the reactions of the 'natives'—that is, the Arabs who formed more than 90 per cent of the population—and, if so, did they think they mattered? There are several pieces of evidence to help answer these questions. One is that the first draft of the Declaration prepared by the Zionist Organisation at Balfour's invitation foresaw the creation of an autonomous Jewish state under the protection of one of the Allied powers. It was after the strong protests of the Jewish Conjoint Committee, representing British Jewry, backed by Edwin Montagu, that the draft was changed to refer to the establishment of a national home for the Jewish people in Palestine, adding the words 'it being clearly understood that nothing shall be done which may prejudice the civil and religious rights of existing non-Jewish communities in Palestine or the rights and political status enjoyed by Jews in any other country.' But, as Balfour was undoubtedly aware, a Jewish national state was what the Zionists wanted.

An Admitted Commitment to Zionism

In his efforts to persuade the war cabinet, Balfour said the Declaration 'did not necessarily involve the early establishment of an independent Jewish state, which was a matter of gradual development in accordance with the ordinary laws of political evolution.' But, being a philosopher more than a politician, Balfour could be unusually candid. In August 1919 he wrote a memorandum on Syria, Palestine and Mesopotamia in which he said:

> The contradiction between the letter of the Covenant and the policy of the Allies is even more flagrant in the case of the independent nation of Palestine than in that of the independent nation of Syria. For in Palestine we do not propose even to go through the form of consulting the wishes of the present inhabitants of the country, though the American Commission [the 1919 King-Crane Commission] has been through the form of asking what they are. The four great powers are committed to Zionism, and Zionism, be it right or wrong, good or bad, is rooted in age-long tradition, in present needs, in future hopes of far profounder import than the desires and prejudices [sic] of 700,000 Arabs who now inhabit that ancient land.

He went on to say that in his opinion this was quite right but that he did not see how this policy could be harmonised with all the other declarations and pledges that had been made by the Allies. 'In fact, so far as Palestine is concerned, the powers have made no statement of fact that is not admittedly wrong, and no declaration of policy which, at least in the letter, they have not always intended to violate.'

The Relevance of Incompatible Pledges

> **"**Israelis celebrate, while Arabs mourn, the anniversary of the Declaration.**"**

A rare and remarkable confession, apart from the Allies' general pledges to set up national governments in the Middle East which would derive their authority 'from the free exercise and choice of the indigenous population', the British government had committed itself in two other ways. One was in the correspondence in 1915 between Sir Henry McMahon, the British High Commissioner in Cairo, and the Sherif Hussain of Mecca, the leader of the Arab revolt against the Turks, and the other was the so-called Sykes-Picot agreement, an Anglo-French understanding on the partition of the Middle East into great-power spheres of influence, which was published by the Russians, to the acute embarrassment of the Allies, after October 1917.

Fountains of ink have flowed in the discussion of how far the British government was to blame for making these pledges which, though couched in ambiguous and evasive language, were undeniably incompatible with each other. Evidence which has recently come to light proves fairly conclusively that at least the Foreign Office believed that the Sherif Hussain had been promised that Palestine should be an independent Arab state.

The question is whether this has any relevance to the present day [1967]. Israelis celebrate, while Arabs mourn, the anniversary of the Declaration, but does it mean any more than, say, the British and French attitudes to Agincourt [a controversial British victory in the Hundred Years' War]? The answer is surely yes. It is sometimes said that, whatever the rights or wrongs of the past, the Zionists have taken Palestine, the Arabs have lost and should recognise the fact, just as Germany will have to forget about her eastern provinces. But the peculiar nature of Zionism invalidates this agreement. What the Arabs remember is that out of this small begin-

British prime minister Arthur James Balfour was responsible for the Balfour Declaration of 1917, which was a pledge of British support for the creation of a Jewish homeland in Palestine. At that time, the area of Palestine had a large Arab population. (**Bob Thomas/Popperfoto/ Getty Images.**)

ning—a brief letter from the British Foreign Secretary to a prominent English Jew—a 9-percent minority in Palestine grew in 30 years to establish its own exclusive and powerful nation-state on land which had been theirs for 1,500 years. They can be forgiven for regarding Zionism as expansionist by nature—especially when Zionists reassert their aim of gathering in the Diaspora of 12 million Jews. Possibly the Palestinian Arabs would have done better to settle for half a loaf by accepting almost any of the proposals for the partition of their country which were made during the British mandate. But would they? It is hard to imagine that Zionism would have been content to live within even narrower frontiers than it occupied in June [1967]. And Britain was incapable of seeing that it did.

The United States Has a Responsibility for the Israeli– Palestinian Problem

Richard H. Curtiss

In the following viewpoint, Richard H. Curtiss contends that the United States is largely responsible for the Israeli-Palestinian problem, including the exodus of Palestinians from their lands and the ensuing Arab-Israeli wars. The United States pushed for partition of Palestine in the United Nations in 1947 even though American diplomats stationed in the Middle East and other government officials cautioned against it. The United States compounded the problem by ignoring the arguments of the secretary and undersecretary of state and other members of the State Department against recognizing the new Jewish state before it agreed to the borders the United Nations assigned it. Richard H. Curtiss is the executive editor of the *Washington Report on*

SOURCE. Richard H. Curtiss, "Truman Adviser Recalls May 14, 1948 US Decision to Recognize Israel," *Washington Report on Middle East Affairs*, May-June 1991, p. 17. Copyright © 1991 American Educational Trust. All rights reserved. Reproduced by permission.

Middle Eastern Affairs. A former U.S. Foreign Service officer and a cofounder of the American Educational Trust, he has authored two books on U.S.–Middle East relations.

With US President George [H.W.] Bush increasingly frustrated by the Israeli-Palestinian problem, a new generation of Americans is asking an old question: Why must the US deal with this seemingly intractable dispute?

The answer, unfortunately, is that the US is largely responsible for the problem because of two American decisions in 1947 and 1948. Now, only the US can break the impasse, by forcing its Israeli client state to give back all or most of the land the United Nations allotted to Muslim and Christian inhabitants when it partitioned Palestine in 1947. . . .

Most people who knew the Middle East at first hand opposed the partition plan, adopted by the United Nations on November 29, 1947. Patently unfair, it awarded 56 percent of Palestine to its 650,000 Jewish inhabitants, and 44 percent to its 1,300,000 Muslim and Christian Arab inhabitants.

Partition was adopted only after ruthless arm-twisting by the US government and by 26 pro-Zionist US senators who, in telegrams to a number of UN member states, warned that US goodwill in rebuilding their World War II–devastated economies might depend on a favorable vote for partition.

In a Nov. 10, 1945 meeting with American diplomats brought in from their posts in the Middle East to urge [President Harry] Truman not to heed Zionist urgings, Truman had bluntly explained his motivation:

> Extensive fighting broke out between Jews and Arabs, just as US diplomats had predicted.

"I'm sorry, gentlemen, but I have to answer to hundreds of thousands who are anxious for the success of

Zionism: I do not have hundreds of thousands of Arabs among my constituents."

Immediately after the plan was adopted, however, extensive fighting broke out between Jews and Arabs, just as US diplomats had predicted. The Arab states categorically rejected the partition by outside parties of an overwhelmingly Arab land.

David Ben-Gurion, soon to be Israel's first prime minister, had ordered his representatives at the UN to accept the plan, but not to enter into any discussion or agreement defining the new Jewish state's borders. . . .

> "Officials in the State Department had done everything in their power to prevent, thwart, or delay the President's Palestine policy in 1947 and 1948."

UN Trusteeship as a Solution

As well-organized Jewish militias seized village after village assigned by the UN plan to the Arabs, and badly organized Arab villagers retaliated with bloody but purposeless attacks on Jewish vehicles and convoys, Secretary of State George C. Marshall urged Truman to reconsider.

The British Army was resolved to withdraw from Palestine on May 15, 1948 regardless of the outcome of events in the UN. The fighting was spreading all over the mandate, including Jerusalem, which was supposed to remain a "corpus separatum" [separate body] under international control and not be assigned either to the Jewish or the Arab state.

Marshall and a majority of diplomats at the UN saw a direct UN trusteeship, succeeding the British mandate, as the only solution to halt the bloodshed. Otherwise, they knew, neighboring Arab states would send military units across the border into Palestine the day the British withdrew, in an attempt to reoccupy the Arab towns and villages seized by Jewish forces. The State Department urged Truman not to grant diplomatic recognition to

Standing alongside Haim Weizman (right), U.S. President Harry S. Truman holds a Torah scroll given to him by the Zionist leader in Washington. Truman chose to recognize the new state of Israel almost immediately after its establishment. (AP Images.)

the Jewish state when the British withdrew, but instead to side with rapidly growing sentiment in the United Nations in favor of trusteeship. Truman wavered and, for a time, both sides in a bitter battle for the president's ear thought they had his support. . . .

Opposition to the President's Palestine Policy

Confirming charges by "Arabists" that the decision to recognize Israel was hasty and based upon domestic political considerations, [Truman's principal domestic advisor Clark] Clifford writes [in a *New Yorker* article]:

> Marshall firmly opposed American recognition of the new Jewish state; I did not. Marshall's opposition was shared by almost every member of the brilliant and now legendary group of presidential advisers, later referred to as the Wise Men, who were then in the process of creating a post-war foreign policy that would endure for more than 40 years. . . .
>
> Officials in the State Department had done everything in their power to prevent, thwart, or delay the President's Palestine policy in 1947 and 1948, while I had fought for assistance to the Jewish Agency.
>
> At midnight on May 14, 1948 (6 PM in Washington), the British would relinquish control of Palestine, which they had been administering under a mandate from the old League of Nations since the First World War. One minute later, the Jewish Agency, under the leadership of David Ben-Gurion, would proclaim the new state. . . .
>
> On May 7th, a week before the end of the British mandate, I met with President Truman for our customary. private day-end chat . . .
>
> I handed the president a draft of a public statement I had prepared, and proposed that at his next press conference, scheduled for May 13th, the day before the British mandate would end, he announce that it was his intention to recognize the Jewish state. The president was sympathetic to the proposal, but, being keenly aware of Marshall's strong feelings, he picked up the telephone to get the Secretary's views. . . .
>
> On ending the conversation, the president swiveled his chair toward me. "Clark, I am impressed with General Marshall's argument that we should not recognize the new state so fast," he said. "He does not want to recognize it at all—at least, not now. I've asked him and [undersecretary of state Robert] Lovett to come in next

> 'We should strengthen [the new Jewish state] in its infancy by prompt recognition.'

week to discuss this business. I think Marshall is going to continue to take a very strong position. . . ."

A Crucial Meeting

At 4 PM on Wednesday, May 12 . . . seven of us joined President Truman in the Oval Office . . . President Truman did not raise the issue of recognition; his desire was that I be the first to raise it, but only after Marshall and Lovett had spoken, so that he would be able to ascertain the degree of Marshall's opposition before showing his own hand.

Lovett began by criticizing what he termed signs of growing "assertiveness" by the Jewish Agency . . . Marshall interrupted Lovett. He was strongly opposed to the behavior of the Jewish Agency, he said. He had met on May 8th with Moshe Shertok, its political representative, and had told Shertok that it was "dangerous to base long-range policy on temporary military success." Moreover, Marshall said, he had told Shertok that if the Jews got into trouble and "came running to us for help . . . there was no warrant to expect help from the United States, which had warned them of the grave risk which they were running." . . . The United States, he said, should continue to support those resolutions in the United Nations which would turn Palestine over to the UN as a trusteeship, and defer any decision on recognition.

Clifford then relates his own arguments, citing the British Balfour Declaration of 1917 promising a Jewish homeland, the European Holocaust, and the possibility of establishing "a nation committed to the democratic system" in the Middle East.

"The new Jewish state can be such a place," Clifford reports he told the group. "We should strengthen it in its infancy by prompt recognition. . . .

Lovett joined the attack. "It would be highly injurious to the United Nations to announce the recognition of the Jewish state even before it had come into existence and while the General Assembly is still considering the question." . . .

Clifford's article details at length his further negotiations, through Undersecretary of State Robert Lovett, to stick to his own plan to recognize the Jewish state. . . .

In recounting this, however, Clifford indicates throughout the *New Yorker* article that he represented President Truman's own personal position, even when he did not consult the president.

Truman's own accounts, . . . and those of his biographers, indicate that he vacillated and was honestly confused. He was pulled one way by Jewish White House adviser David Niles, and Truman's old Jewish army buddy and business partner, Eddie Jacobson, and another by the professionals at the State Department.

Setting the Machinery in Motion

Meanwhile Clifford and Niles, as well as the Department of State, were dealing directly with Eliahu Epstein, the Jewish Agency (predecessor to the government of Israel) representative in Washington. Clifford describes his own role on May 14 as follows:

Even without a clear signal from Lovett and Marshall, I felt, we had to set in motion the machinery for recognition, in the event that a favorable decision was made. At 10 am, I made a different call—one that I looked on later with great pleasure. . . .

"Mr. Epstein," I told the Jewish Agency representative, "we would like you to send an official letter to President Truman before 12 o'clock today formally requesting the United States to recognize the new Jewish state. I would also request that you send a copy of the letter directly to Secretary Marshall."

Epstein was ecstatic. He did not realize that the president had still not decided how to respond to the request I had just solicited. . . . It was particularly important, I said, that the new state claim nothing beyond the boundaries outlined in the UN resolution of Nov. 29, 1947, because those boundaries were the only ones that had been agreed to. . . .

A few minutes later, Epstein called me. "We've never done this before, and we're not quite sure how to go about it," he said. . . . With my knowledge and encouragement, Epstein then turned for additional advice to two of the wisest lawyers in Washington, David Ginsburg and Benjamin Cohen, both of whom were great New Dealers and strong supporters of the Zionist cause. Working together during the rest of the morning, he and they drafted the recognition request. . . .

> "Five Arab-Israeli wars . . . and the Middle East instability . . . are largely attributable to US recognition of Israel before it officially agreed to the borders assigned it by the United Nations in 1947."

The Ongoing Impact of US Recognition

Clifford closes with the well-known story of how a Jewish Agency employee driving to the White House with the request for recognition of "the Jewish state" was overhauled by another Jewish Agency employee. Epstein had just heard on the radio that the new state was to be called "Israel" and instructed the second employee to write in that name in ink before handing over the request for recognition to the White House.

Meanwhile, General Marshall agreed that, although he could not support President Truman on the issue, he would not oppose it. When the news was broken to the American delegation at the UN, which had been lining up votes for continued trusteeship, US Ambassador Warren Austin left the building in order not to be present when US recognition of Israel was announced, just 11 minutes after the state's creation. . . . [Clifford writes:]

> Lovett remained adamant for the rest of his life, however, in his view that the president and I had been wrong. So did most of his colleagues. . . . Because President Truman was often annoyed by the tone and fierceness of the pressure exerted on him by American Zionists, he left some people with the impression that he was ambivalent about the events of May 1948. This was not true. He never wavered in his belief that he had taken the right action.

Nor, apparently, does Clifford, who never once expresses any regret about the 750,000 Palestinians pushed out of their country during the 1947 to 1949 fighting, and never allowed by Israel to return to their homes. Nor does Clifford seem to realize that his opponents in the bureaucratic battle he describes are vindicated by the five Arab-Israeli wars. These and the Middle East instability that has led to the overthrow of several Arab governments and, perhaps, the two bloody wars in the Persian Gulf, are largely attributable to US recognition of Israel before it officially agreed to the borders assigned it by the United Nations in 1947. That recognition has led subsequently to the US military and economic support of every elected government of Israel.

Palestinian Arabs Should Be Returned to Their Homes

Rafat Abu Ghali

In the following viewpoint, Rafat Abu Ghali maintains that the solution to the Palestinian refugee problem is to give the refugees back their original land, reimburse them for the losses they suffered as a result of the creation of the state of Israel, and punish those who committed terrible crimes against them. He relates incidents that led his family and other Arab Palestinians to flee their homes and begin new lives as refugees. He goes on to describe how the *Nakba*, the defeat and destruction of Palestinian society in 1948, affected and has continued to affect the lives of Palestinian refugees. Rafat Abu Ghali is a Palestinian refugee who lives in the Al-Shabora refugee camp in the Gaza Strip. He is a full-time lecturer at the Palestinian Al-Aqsa University.

SOURCE. Rafat Abu Ghali, "The Darker it Is, the Closer We Are to the Break of Dawn," *al majdal*, Winter-Spring 2008, pp. 45–47. Copyright © 1998–2007 badil.org. All rights reserved. Reproduced by permission.

My family's name is Abu Ghali and my family comes from Bir Saba. We used to own 48,000 sq meters of cultivatable land. People used to cultivate their land in winter and move to another area called Sidna Ali, near Jaffa. There, they used to rent land lots and cultivate them. During the harvest season they would go back to Bir Saba. In 1933, the British came and expelled the Arabs from Sidna Ali in order to settle Jewish immigrants on their lands. They offered compensation to the land owners. The compensation was one camel, twelve cans of oils, and 20,000 sq meters of land with a house built on it in the Moqibla area near Jenin. Most people accepted the offer, among them was Khalil Abu Ghali, my grandfather. Those who rejected the offer were expelled by force. A Jewish settlement called Kabus was built there.

The Zionist schemes started in Tel Aviv and Jaffa. Arab owners understood the real intention of these schemes;

As a Palestinian flag flaps in the background, a Palestinian boy in Jabalia refugee camp in the northern Gaza Strip walks atop the rubble of his house. It was destroyed during Israel's 22-day offensive there on March 1, 2009. (Mahmud Hams/ AFP/Getty Images.)

> Zionist forces hunted down the Palestinians to kill them while they were escaping to Gaza.

they were offered two-storey houses built on Palestinian lands. According to the plan, the ground floor was to be occupied by Palestinian land owners while the first floor was for Jewish immigrants. When violence erupted, the Jewish residents started firing from the first floor on their Palestinian neighbors. The British did not allow Arabs to own guns, but they provided weapons for the Jews.

Growing Violence

The Zionist forces secretly brought four trucks loaded with weapons for military training and armament, but were seen by a Palestinian man living in the area. The man was from the Shawabka clan, and his clan received death threats from the Zionists, who told them not to tell anyone about the weapons they saw or they would all be killed. The British were informed and confiscated the weapons without punishing the Zionists. One day later, Zionist forces attacked the homes of the Shawabka clan, killing five people. While Khalil Abu Ghali was going to sell his orange harvest in Ramat Gan, he saw dead people lying on the ground and injured people. Their relatives, from the Shawabka clan, were crying in anger. He went back home because he was afraid to be killed by the Zionists. This is also the reason why he left to Gaza with his family and relatives. Some of his relatives went to Gaza while others went to Jenin in the West Bank. Zionist forces hunted down the Palestinians to kill them while they were escaping to Gaza.

There was a notable incident which involved the poisoning of a water well. People saw Zionists put poison in the well and removed the poison bottle immediately. They tried hard to purify the water but were unsuccessful. My grandfather, Khalil Abu Ghali, came to fill twelve jars of water from the well but people told him not to do so because the well had been poisoned. Unfortunately, he thought people did not want him to fill his jars to keep the water for themselves and their livestock. He filled his jars and paid no attention to their warnings. He took the water to his family

> [My family] moved from the very top to the very bottom overnight.

who used the water for drinking in the evening. The following morning, everyone from his family fell ill and started vomiting; especially Khalil's 12 year-old daughter, Tamam. She went into a coma and died instantly. However, Tamam was not the only victim. Other people died and some suffered from hair loss because of the poisoned water. Those who drank camel milk recovered soon while people who refused to drink it stayed in hospital for two months for treatment. They left the area and moved to another area called Hirb Thiab.

The planes started bombing Gaza and people were forced to move towards Al-Bureij camp in Gaza. The Zionists kept hunting them down. People had to run to Rafah and stayed there ever since. All of my family members are registered refugees with UNRWA [United Nations Relief and Works Agency for Palestine Refugees in the Near East]. They benefited from the food rations that UNRWA used to give to Palestinian refugees in the early years after 1948.

Effects of the Nakba

The Nakba ["catastrophe"] affected us very badly. We lost everything. It was a dramatic change for our family. We moved from the very top to the very bottom overnight. We were living on our own lands, growing our crops and breeding livestock. We used to depend on organic crops and livestock. We became homeless refugees, waiting for other nations to give us something to eat. We still tell our children about our land. They know their original land very well. It is inscribed in our hearts and minds.

Being a refugee means a lot to me. Being a refugee, I cannot forget that I have rights to fight for. It means that my family and I are looking forward to regaining our stolen land from the oppressors.

Socially, one of the main impacts of the Nakba is that the differences between people from different villages and towns melted away. In many places, marriage used to take place only within the same clan or village. Nowadays people marry their daughters to people from distant places and clans. The Nakba also changed our professions. We were land owners and farmers. We were less educated then. Now we work as teachers, doctors, engineers, mechanics, nurses, social workers, and builders. We changed our professions because we were forced to, in order to adapt to the new living conditions associated with our situation as refugees in Gaza.

A Just Solution to the Refugee Problem

I studied English in India. I chose this profession because of the job market. There has been a need for English teachers in Gaza. I worked for the armed forces for a while as a translator but I did not like it. I felt that teaching at university is better and more rewarding in terms of academic status and professional development. Currently I am working at Al-Aqsa University as a full time lecturer. I live in Shabora refugee camp in Rafah. I live there because it is the place my parents came as refugees 60 years ago.

> The solution is simple: return the refugees to their original land and compensate them for their losses.

There has been a misconception about solving the refugee problem. The international community has always been ambivalent when it comes to Palestinians. The solution is simple: return the refugees to their original land and compensate them for their losses. One state solution is fine, but we do not want to be second class citizens living under a colonial power. Jews, Christians and

Muslims can live side by side, but the last word should be for Palestinians, the indigenous people of Palestine. Criminals who committed heinous crimes against us should face justice as well.

A just solution means the return of rights, all rights and the punishment of all criminals. The responses of the UN and other international organizations were nice to look at and read, but they were never applied. They cannot be applied when they concern the rights of Palestinians such as the right of return. Why don't we have a UNHCR [United Nations High Commissioner for Refugees] in Palestine? I think that the UN and other international bodies are accomplices by being silent. Why does the UN use force in other places of the world and not here? We need more than words and humanitarian aid from the UN and the international community.

A Desperate Need for a Change

As for the peace process, it is not effective enough for us. The Israelis have left Gaza but they are still bombing us from the sky. We live in the prison where we were born; no movement, no travel, no leisure, no security, nothing at all! We miss a lot of the basic things which are available to all free nations.

I do not know what will happen to me or to my children. Our best weapon is education, which is, unfortunately, deteriorating. We have to stick hard to our books and pencils because education is the only effective weapon to fight the occupation. My slogan is Education! Education—in order to face occupation.

Sometimes I think that our kids have a bleak future. There is not enough space in the Gaza strip. People are suffering now and life is worse than ever. We are living under the most extraordinarily difficult circumstances. I think, however, that the darker it is, the closer we are to the break of dawn. The situation cannot remain as bad as it is now.

Palestinian Arabs Should Not Have the Right of Return

Rachel Neuwirth

In the following viewpoint, Rachel Neuwirth argues that Palestinians should not have the "right of return." Palestinian Arabs were the primary aggressors, not innocent victims, in the 1948 war, she contends. She asserts that Palestinians did not evacuate because Israeli leaders ordered them to do so. They fled because Arab leaders and governments told them they should. Many refugees claiming that their land must be returned to them never owned land in Palestine, Neuwirth notes, and others only lived there a very short time. Still others are descendents of Arab Palestinians and have never themselves lived in Palestine, she contends. Many other refugees from war or revolution in other lands were not granted right of return, and the Palestinian Arabs should not be granted a right those others were not, she maintains. Rachel Neuwirth is a political com-

SOURCE. Rachel Neuwirth, "The Arab 'Right of Return' to Israel," *American Thinker*, January 6, 2008. Copyright © 2008 American Thinker. Reproduced by permission.

mentator and analyst who specializes in the Middle East with particular emphasis on militant Islam and Israeli foreign policy.

A media and propaganda campaign has been under way . . . to legitimate the longstanding demands made on behalf of the Palestinian "Arab refugees"—meaning in practice the grandchildren and great-grandchildren of refugees—from the 1948 Arab-Israel war of 60 years ago, for their return to their ancestral homes and the return of all their ancestors' former land and property in what is now Israel.

The Palestinian National Authority headed by Mahmoud Abbas and the Palestinian Liberation Organization founded by Yasser Arafat have always made this demand a *sine qua non* [absolutely essential] for "peace" with Israel. . . . And the Palestinian Arab leadership continues to stand by this demand today, promising their supporters that they will never agree to "peace" without its acceptance by Israel.

> 'The rights of the Palestinian refugees have been ignored for six decades by a world that has wished them away.'

Media Support for the Right of Return

An example of the current media blitz on behalf of this "right of return" demand is an op-ed by Nir Rosen, a reporter who has covered the Islamic world for many of the United States' leading media organs, in the *Washington Post*. Mr. Rosen writes:

The rights of the Palestinian refugees have been ignored for six decades by a world that has wished them away. But the Middle East will never know peace or stability until they are granted justice. In 1948–49, around the conflict that Israelis refer to as their War of Independence and that Palestinians call the Catastrophe, some 750,000

Palestinians were ethnically cleansed to make way for the creation of the Jewish state. In 1967, during the Six-Day War, 400,000 Palestinians were expelled by the Israeli military, according to Amnesty International.

A similar polemic by one Ghada Ageel, who describes herself as "a third-generation Palestinian refugee [who] grew up in the Khan Yunis refugee camp in Gaza and teaches Middle Eastern politics at the University of Exeter in Britain," appeared in the Dec.1, 2007 issue of the *Los Angeles Times*: Ms. Ageel avers:

> Sixty years ago, my grandparents lived in the beautiful village of Beit Daras, a few kilometers north of Gaza. They were farmers and owned hundreds of acres of land. But in 1948, in the first Arab-Israeli war, many people lost their lives defending our village from the Zionist militias. In the end, with their crops and homes burning, the villagers fled. . . . We became refugees, queuing for tents, food and assistance, while the state of Israel was established on the ruins of my family's property and on the ruins of hundreds of other Palestinian villages. . . . I raise this story today . . . to help convey the deep-seated fears of Palestinian refugees that we will be asked to exonerate Israel for its actions and to relinquish our right to return home. That cannot be allowed to happen. All refugees have the right to return. This is an individual right, long recognized in international law, that cannot be negotiated away.

In Defense of the Israelis

What is wrong with these demands? Just about everything. Here are only a few of the reasons why they are unjust, ill-intentioned and grounded in deceit:

First and foremost, the Palestinian Arabs were the primary *aggressors* in the 1948 war, not innocent victims of the "Zionists" as their spokesmen and advocates claim.

The Palestinian Arab guerilla-terrorists used very brutal tactics indeed in 1947–48 to achieve their leaders' publicly affirmed goal of "driving the Jews into the sea." . . .

Soon terrorist and guerilla attacks on Jewish villages and urban neighborhoods were being carried out all across Palestine. Few if any Jewish communities were spared attack. . . . The attacks on Jewish-operated vehicles along the roads were especially vicious, resulting in many casualties and effectively closing all of the major roads in Palestine to Jewish traffic.

> Many Arab leaders . . . have confirmed the role of the Palestinian Arab leadership and the governments of the Arab states in causing the mass evacuation of much of the Arab population.

As a result, many Jewish communities developed severe shortages of food, fuel, and medicines. The Jerusalem areas' 100,000 Jewish inhabitants were especially hard-hit by the Palestinian Arabs' siege warfare. By May 15, 1948, after five and a half months of Palestinian guerilla-terrorist attacks, but *before* six Arab states had begun their massive invasion of Palestine-Israel, 2,500 Jews had already been killed, half of them civilians, and thousands more had been wounded. . . .

By the time the war ended, about 6,000 Jews had been killed, including approximately 2,000 civilians—nearly one per cent of the Jewish population of Palestine/Israel.

In order to defend the country's 650,000 Jewish inhabitants, whose villages and urban neighborhoods were scattered amongst Arab ones, from annihilation by the combined Palestinian Arab and Arab states' onslaught, the Palestinian Jewish defense militias . . . were forced to capture Palestinian villages that served as bases of operation for the guerilla-terrorist attackers. It is true that when the defense militias entered some Palestinian villages in order to drive out or capture the guerilla-terrorists, much of the Palestinian Arab civilian population also fled from these villages. . . .

The Arab Palestinian guerillas did not wear uniforms or distinguish themselves in any way from the Arab civilian population, among whom they lived and from whom they were recruited. As a result, there was no way that the Israeli soldiers could drive the guerillas out of these villages without adversely affecting their noncombatant relatives and neighbors.

Arab Responsibility for Palestinian Exodus

Even so, the Israeli forces' counter-guerilla operations . . . , were not even the immediate cause of the "exodus" of most Palestinian Arabs from the areas that became Israel in 1948. Many Arab leaders as well as ordinary Palestinian Arabs have confirmed the role of the Palestinian Arab leadership and the governments of the Arab states in causing the mass evacuation of much of the Arab population from what is now Israel. . . . A prime example is none other than the present head of the Palestinian Authority, Mahmoud Abbas (Abu Mazen). Abbas wrote in March 1976 that

> the Arab armies entered Palestine to protect the Palestinians from the Zionist tyranny, but instead they abandoned them, forced them to emigrate and to leave their homeland, imposed upon them a political and ideological blockade and threw them into prisons similar to the ghettos in which the Jews used to live in Eastern Europe.

Another well-informed Arab politician, Khaled al-Azm, a former Syrian Prime Minister, states in his memoirs published in 1973 that

> since 1948, it is we who have demanded the return of the refugees, while it is we who made them leave. We brought disaster upon a million Arab refugees by inviting them and bringing pressure on them to leave. We

Many peoples have been forced from their homelands, their land seized without compensation, because of wars and revolutions since the start of the 20th century. Such refugees include the Hmong, who fled Laos for Thailand in the mid-1970s, and relocated in the United States for a new life under a resettlement program launched by the U.S. government. (©Paula Bronstein/Getty Images.)

have accustomed them to begging. . . . We have participated in lowering their morale and social level. . . . Then we exploited them in executing crimes of murder, arson and throwing stones upon men, women and children . . . all this in the service of political purposes. . . .

And Mahmud Al-Habbash, a columnist for the . . . paper, *Al-Hayat Al-Jadida,* has confirmed that the Arabs left Israel in 1948 only after Arab leaders persuaded them to do so by promising them a speedy return to their homes in Palestine; as Habbash puts it,

the leaders and the elites promised us at the beginning of the 'Catastrophe' [the establishment of Israel and the creation of the refugee problem] in 1948, that the duration of the exile will not be long, and that it will not last more than a few days or months, and afterwards the refugees will return to their homes, which most of them did not

leave only until they put their trust in those . . . promises
made by the leaders and the political elites. . . .

In Dispute of Arab Claims

Even the claims of many of the present-day "refugees"
to be Palestinians are dubious. In her painstakingly
researched study *From Time Immemorial,* Joan Peters
points out that UNRWA [United Nations Relief and
Works Agency for Palestine Refugees in the Near East]
defines [as a refugee] any Arab who lived in Palestine
for a minimum of only two years before Israel became
independent in 1948, and who left Israeli territory at that
time, plus all Arabs descended from such individuals to
the end of time. As Ms. Peters documents at great length,
tens if not hundreds of thousands of Arabs immigrated
to Palestine under the British Mandate administration
of 1918–1948, attracted by the massive economic development and infrastructure improvements introduced
into Palestine by the Jewish "settlers" and the British
administration.

Thus many of the "Palestinians" not only have never
lived in Palestine themselves, but are fairly distant descendants of people who lived their only briefly before 1948,
having been born elsewhere in the Arab world. . . .

Dubious are the claims of so many of the refugees
to be the heirs of former Palestinian landowners. . . .
Very few Palestinian Arabs actually left behind valuable
property when they left Israeli territory in 1948. Prior to
Israel's independence very few Arabs possessed clear and
unencumbered legal title to land in Palestine. Vast areas
of the country were the property of the "state" (originally
the Turkish government). Other land was held in common by villages.

Much of what land as was privately owned by Arabs
prior to 1948 was included in vast latifundia [great
landed estates] owned by a few dozen wealthy "effendi"
(aristocratic) families, some of whom did not even live

Making Aliyah Possible for All

Aliyah refers to the immigration of Jewish individuals to Israel, and this movement has continued, legally and illegally, since it began in the late 19th century. Since 2002, a Jerusalem based organization called Nefesh B'Nefesh (NBN) has sought potential Jewish immigrants, or Olim, in North America and the United Kingdom. NBN's mission is

> to revitalize Western Aliyah and expand it for generations to come, by removing the financial, professional and bureaucratic obstacles that are preventing many potential Olim from fulfilling their dreams. In the process, we hope to send an unmistakable signal of Jewish solidarity linking Israel and the Diaspora.

That Diaspora includes all countries, outside of the Holy Land, that are now housing people of Jewish descent. Even after the creation of the state of Israel in 1948, the majority of the Jewish population still lives in the Diaspora.

Nefesh B'Nefesh attempts to ease some of the burdens of Aliyah by subsidizing travel; aiding in job, school, and housing searches; and supporting the emotional transitions for individuals and families.

in Palestine. Most Palestinian Arabs were tenant farmers, landless laborers, or Bedouin nomads. And such farms as were owned by Arab smallholders were usually hard-scrabble affairs on sandy, unproductive soil, which enabled their cultivators at most to eke out a bare living. Their owners were heavily indebted to money-lenders or large landlords.

In addition, many Arabs who claim to have once owned land in Palestine were actually squatters on pre-

> Why should the Palestinian Arabs be considered a uniquely special case, with more rights than other refugees from wars and/or revolutions?

viously unoccupied and unclaimed "state" land, without a legal private owner. Although many of these individuals never possessed title deeds to the land they professed to own and did not pay any taxes on them, they or their descendants nonetheless demand that "their" land be "returned" to them.

Claims of massive poverty, deprivation and suffering on the part of the Palestinian Arab refugees are largely false. For sixty years four generations of Palestinian refugees or alleged refugees have had all or most of their housing, food, education through college and graduate school, medical care and social services provided to them for free by UNRWA. . . .

There have been no tents in the "refugee camps" (actually towns or urban neighborhoods) since the 1950s; the "refugees" live in apartments or houses, many of them as large and with the same amenities as apartments and houses in the United States and Europe. . . .

Right of Return Is Unwarranted

The international community has not recognized or enforced a "right of return" for most of the very numerous non-Palestinian refugee communities throughout the world. The list of refugee populations who have been forced from their homelands and whose lands have been seized without compensation because of wars and revolutions within the past 100 years is endless. The more than 850,000 Jews who have either been expelled or fled from Arab and other Muslim countries since the Arab world initiated hostilities against the Jews of Israel-Palestine in 1947; the fifteen million Germans expelled from Pomerania, Silesia, Bohemia and Moravia by Poland and Czechoslovakia after World War II; the two million ethnic Greeks and Turks who were expelled from either Greece or Turkey in a "population exchange" administered by the League of Nations in 1922; the additional 200,000 Greeks who were expelled from northern Cyprus by the Turkish military invasion in 1974; the millions of Hindus who fled the newly created Muslim state of "Pakistan" and the millions of Muslims who fled what remained of India to Pakistan following the partition of India in 1947; the millions of Russians who fled Russia after the Communist takeover of that country in 1917 for other European countries or the United States; and the millions of Cubans, Vietnamese and Laotians who fled their homelands for the United States after the Communist take-overs of these countries, have all been denied repatriation, the return of the vast amounts of property they were forced to leave behind, or even compensation for their lost property.

Why should the Palestinian Arabs be considered a uniquely special case, with more rights than other refugees from wars and/or revolutions? . . .

It is long overdue for the libel [false publication] of an Israeli or Zionist "original sin" against the Palestinian Arabs to be discredited, along with the supposed Palestinian Arab "right of return," which is grounded in this false "narrative."

CHAPTER 3

Personal Narratives

A Briton Serves in Palestine from 1946 to 1948

Howard Mansfield

In the following viewpoint, Howard Mansfield describes his experiences as a member of the British section of the Palestine police during the last years of the British Mandate and shortly after. He describes the Muslim town of Nablus, its police facilities, and its people and relates how the situation in the town changed after the United Nations voted in favor of partition and the establishment of a Jewish state in Palestine. He goes on to depict life and conditions in conflict-torn Jerusalem, where he was posted next, and then in Haifa, where he stayed until the end of June 1948. Mansfield was one of the last members of the British section of the Palestine police to leave the country after the end of the British Mandate in Palestine.

Photo on previous page: A cave in the hills east of Bethlehem is home to Mohamed Ahmed Issa and his family of seven. Many Arab families such as Issa's fled their homes in the territory that became Israel in the late 1940s. (**AP Images.**)

SOURCE. Howard Mansfield, "British Mandate: On Duty in Nablus, Jerusalem and Haifa from 1946–1948." Reproduced by permission.

My first posting in the Palestine Police was to Nablus in an area steeped in Biblical history. . . .

Nablus was the administrative capital of the District of Samaria, boasting a District Officer, a District Police Headquarters, a rural police station, which was entirely mounted, a district jail, and an urban police station housing British and Arab members of the Palestine Police. I was posted to Nablus Urban. . . .

We patrolled the town paired with an Arab policeman, by night and day, carrying out normal peace-time police duties, and although there was no terrorism or political unrest of the kind that the Jewish areas were experiencing we carried Lee Enfield (SMLE) rifles and a cloth bandolier of 50 rounds of .303 ammunition for our own protection. . . .

After a few months of patrol duties I was moved to the Investigation Section which brought me into much closer contact with the Arab policemen and the townspeople and villagers. . . .

Nablus was a fervent Moslem stronghold and, in accordance with strict Moslem tradition, the women dressed in black robes and veils when in the town. These robes were not floor-length chadors [Muslim gowns], and some of the younger ladies wore stylish shoes and transparent silk veils revealing well made-up faces. The Bedouin women were completely covered but many had elaborate facial tattoos and strings of gold coins dangling across their faces as a sign of wealth. . . .

> Once the U.N. resolution was adopted the situation in Nablus began to deteriorate.

Both the Urban and the Rural stations at Nablus were part of the network of modern police stations which had been built following a report in 1938 by Sir Charles Tegart, a former Commissioner of Police in Calcutta, who was advising the Inspector General on security matters. They were red sand-stone buildings of the Foreign Legion style of architecture. The smaller Urban stations were a single block, with messing [dining] and sleeping accommodation on the upper floor, while the Mounted stations were built in a square with the stables on one side, the station offices on another, and the Arab and British living accommodation on the other two sides. . . .

The Situation Changes

Numerous bodies had looked into the Palestine situation over the years, and in August 1947 the United Nations Special Committee on Palestine (UNSCOP) submitted its report and recommended that the country be partitioned. The Arabs rejected the recommendation and vowed to resist but never believed that the British would leave. The Jews accepted it with the intention of getting as much territory as they could when the British left. On 29th November 1947 the U.N. General Assembly adopted a Resolution requiring the establishment of a Jewish State in Palestine, and Great Britain announced that the mandate would be terminated on May 15th 1948.

Once the U.N. resolution was adopted the situation in Nablus began to deteriorate. At the beginning of 1948, a group of well-known . . . soldiers of fortune from Lebanon . . . was reported in the area, and the locals began to carry rifles openly in public. The crackle of rifle fire could be heard frequently at night, but at this stage no one was being shot at and the firing was purely the customary morale-boosting exercise. There were no British troops at all in Samaria and the only soldiers we had ever seen were a few members of the Trans-Jordan Frontier Force. . . .

There was still little animosity being shown to us at this stage and when we abruptly left in 3-ton trucks for Jerusalem in late January 1948 the townspeople stood in disbelief. There was only one armoured vehicle at the station, an old pre-war clunker, known as the pig, which

> There were road blocks where we were stopped by poorly trained, very twitchy local militias who considered everyone to be the enemy.

had a hand-cranked revolving turret for firing a rifle or Bren gun [light, gas-powered machine gun] out of. It would not have made the trip to Jerusalem and was left behind at the station in the hands of our Arab police colleagues.

Life in Jerusalem

When we arrived in Jerusalem, my group from Nablus became part of a force of British police which had been organized to help in the withdrawal and to stabilize the situation in the capital. Jerusalem was like a city under siege. All public buildings were heavily sandbagged and guarded, and the only policing that was being done was responding to the numerous terrorist incidents. The police were now equipped with 2-man armoured cars, with radio communications and a Bren gun. These were positioned at crucial points around the city and would race to the scene of an incident, often while it was in progress. As an additional protection the exterior of the armoured cars was electrified to prevent people from climbing up onto them while stationary.

We lived in villas in the German Colony and drove out every morning to key British and Jewish sites to protect them from the terrorists. My most memorable post was manning a Bren gun inside Barclays Bank . . . across from the so-called New Gate in the walls of the walled Old City, to prevent the bank from being robbed. I sat in a sandbagged cupola on the mezzanine looking down at the main counter, waiting for terrorists to strike. Our soft-skinned [i.e., unarmored] vehicles would be fired on as we drove through Jewish areas along the walls of the Old City, but there were no casualties and when we were off duty we were able to live a fairly normal existence.

The chaplain of the Palestine Police was an Irish Franciscan monk called Father Eugene, who was a highly respected personage in Jerusalem and a great guide to the Holy Places. Together, we were able to walk the Stations of the Cross along the Via Dolorosa, and visit the Church of the Holy Sepulchre, the Mount of Olives and the Garden of Gethsemane which were all virtually in our backyard. In spite of the present upheaval, Pax Britannica ["the British peace"] still made it possible for us to mingle with orthodox Jews at the Wailing Wall, with Arabs at the Mosque of Omar on the Dome of the Rock, and with Christians at the birthplace of Christ at the Church of the Nativity in Bethlehem a few miles away.

At this stage we were also able to spend some time in the Jewish Quarters, which had some of the European features which I had missed in almost a year in strict Moslem surroundings. Some of the Jewish bars were reasonably hospitable, and I was having a quiet drink in one of them one evening when the building across the road was blown up. We raced outside and found that the premises of the *Palestine Post* newspaper were on fire. We did what we could to stop the fire from spreading until the Fire Brigade arrived, but it burned all night and the building was completely destroyed. It was rumoured later that this might have been the work of British army deserters.

Preparing for the End of the Mandate

It was not possible for the British army and all its equipment to leave the country in the short time before the end of the mandate, and so to retrieve as much as possible an enclave was set up at the port of Haifa through which the troops and equipment would be withdrawn. Volunteers were called for from the Palestine Police to stay on after the end of the mandate to provide traffic control and security, and I volunteered to stay. Even at that, a large quantity of warlike stores was simply disposed of by driving it over a cliff into the sea. A month before the mandate ended, we received word that we were to withdraw from Jerusalem to Haifa. The briefing was given by the normally taciturn Superintendent, Ian Proud, who was not given to exaggeration. This time his briefing was nothing short of dramatic: the Jews were already taking action to secure the main road from Tel Aviv to Jerusalem, even before the partition date, and roadblocks had been set up by both Jews and Arabs on the route we would be taking. We would be travelling in the usual soft-skinned 3-ton trucks but there would be an armoured car escort and we must be prepared to fight our way through.

Haifa: The End of the Road

All distances in Palestine are small and the journey to Haifa was less than a hundred and fifty kilometres, but the roads through the hills were not good at the best of times and now there were road blocks where we were stopped by poorly trained, very twitchy local militias who considered everyone to be the enemy. It was a slow and tense drive but there were no serious incidents and we were all intact when we arrived at our new quarters, a former monastery south west of Haifa. The Central Police Station had been badly damaged the previous September by a barrel of explosives catapulted over the perimeter fence from the back of a Jewish truck, but the Palestine Police were still nominally in control of the city. As evidence of this, the Station Officer, a man of striking military bearing would stride around his domain every morning, immaculate in his summer uniform with highly polished Sam Browne belt [wide belt with a shoulder strap], all topped by the black astrakhan hat (or kalpak) which senior police officers and Arab policemen wore.

A Haifa Operational Patrol had been formed, whose armoured cars were on immediate alert in the station compound with their engines running and their Bren guns cocked. . . .

> We were obviously a high-risk target.

As the end of the mandate approached, the British police finally handed over the Haifa police stations to the Jewish members of the Palestine Police. The sounds of intense battle had been heard for a few days and we learned that the Jews had already driven many Arabs out of the city. The British no longer had even de facto

In Bethlehem, a British policeman inspects a Palestinian man for weapons, which were illegal for Arabs to possess in the municipal area. (AP Images.)

jurisdiction but in spite of this, my group was given the task of controlling traffic on the main routes of the city through which the army was withdrawing. . . .

The Port of Haifa itself remained entirely under British control even after the mandate had ended and apart from the usual dock thefts there were few security problems. We continued to live in the monastery outside the town, where our own security became a serious concern. Our small arms, including Bren guns, were very much sought after by the now legal terrorist groups and we were obviously a high-risk target. A sand-bagged Bren gun position at the entrance to our compound was manned day and night and patrols roamed inside until we, the last members of the British section of the Palestine Police finally left at the end of June 1948.

A Student Celebrates the Dawn of a Jewish State

Zipporah Porath

In the following viewpoint, written November 30, 1947, the morning after the United Nations voted to approve the Partition Plan for Palestine, American student Zipporah ("Zippy" Borowsky) Porath shares with her family her experiences and the excitement she felt at that time. She relates how she and her fellow students reacted when they first heard the results of the UN vote on the Partition Plan for Palestine. She goes on to describe in detail the celebrations in the streets of Jerusalem, the reactions of the crowds to the speeches of Jewish leaders Golda Myerson (Meir) and David Ben-Gurion, and the overwhelming emotions experienced by her friends and all those they encountered. Zipporah Porath is a writer and lecturer. A native New Yorker, she went to British Mandatory Palestine in 1947 for a year of study at the Hebrew University, and eventually made Israel her home.

SOURCE. Zipporah Porath, "Jerusalem: Sunday Morning, 11:00 A.M., November 30, 1947," From Zipporah Porath's book, *Letters from Jerusalem 1947–1948*, third edition, Jonathan Publications, 2008, pp. 43–47. Copyright © 1987 Zipporah Porath. Reproduced by permission of the author. *To order copies contact:* zip@netvision.net.il *or* jporath@mac.com.

Jerusalem
Sunday morning, 11:00 A.M.
November 30, 1947

Dearest Mother, Dad and Naomi,

I walked in a semi-daze through the crowds of happy faces, through the deafening singing, *"David, Melech Yisrael, chai, chai vekayam"* [David, King of Israel, lives and is alive), past the British tanks and jeeps piled high with pyramids of flag-waving, cheering children. I dodged motor cycles, wagons, cars and trucks which were racing madly up and down King George V Street, missing each other miraculously, their running boards and headlights overflowing with layer upon layer of elated, happy people. I pushed my way past the crying, kissing tumultuous crowds and the exultant shouts of "Mazal Tov" [congratulations] and came back to the quiet of my room . . . to try to share with you this never-to-be-forgotten night.

> We got through just as the announcement of the majority vote was made: thirty-three in favor, thirteen against and ten abstentions.

Victory at the UN

The light in my room was still on from last night. I had planned to go to sleep early since rumor had it that voting at the UN on the Partition Plan would probably be postponed for another day. But, at about 11:00 p.m. there was a knock on the door: "We're getting through to America. Come on down. The voting's tonight." Ten pajama-clad bodies crowded into a room with space enough for five and sat tensely round the battered radio for what seemed like hours while vain attempts were made to get clear reception from Lake Success. We got through just as the announcement of the majority vote was made: thirty-three in favor, thirteen against and ten abstentions.

Ecstatic, we hugged and kissed each other frantically, then stood rigidly at attention and sang *Hatikvah* ["*The Hope*": Israel's national anthem] fervently. Out came bottles of wine, biscuits and candy. We ate and drank and held a solemn little ceremony, then dashed to our rooms, hurriedly slipped on whatever clothing was on hand and banged on all the doors to wake up those who had slept through the good news. All the students in the building scrambled up to the roof and, under the warmth of moonglow and wine, danced deliriously. Then we made a snake line to the nearest houses, banging on the shutters and doors, shouting the news as we went. In a seemingly endless column, we wound our way to the next community, Bet Hakerem, where the Teachers Seminary is and where most of its students live. The streets were already full, ring upon ring of dancing groups circling in a frenzied hora [circle dance]. Ours was the last and largest circle.

Tears of Joy

Arms linked, marching six abreast, singing all the way, the battalion of students advanced, shouting the news to neighbors who poked their sleepy heads out of windows and doors to see what the commotion was about, straight to Hamekasher, the bus terminal. Confronting the watchman with the news, we demanded a bus to take us to town. He was so excited he provided three. In a mad scramble we piled in, body on body; down the road we raced like a million hearts on fire, headed for the heart of Jerusalem.

The streets in the city were beginning to fill as the news got around. People poured out of their homes in a continuous ever thickening stream. In the center of town crowds of happy people, hugging each other, dancing horas and jigs, headed spontaneously,

> " We looked at each other, drew closer together, wrapped arms . . . and felt the thrill of experiencing a historic wonder, dawn bidding Shalom to a Jewish State. "

as we were headed—drawn by some magnetic force—to the courtyard of the fortress-like Sochnut [Jewish Agency] building, which for years housed the hopes for a Jewish State in Palestine. Out came a flag and onto the balcony came Golda Myerson [Meir—head of the Political Department of the Jewish Agency]. There were no words to suit the moment. Choked with emotion, she managed to say "Mazal Tov" and down came tears, oceans of unrestrained happy tears. All night streams of joyful crowds assembled in the courtyard milling in and out—to pay homage, to give vent to exultant feelings that welled up from deep inside.

A Morning of Celebration

A group of us marched to the press room of the *Palestine Post* to get the latest news from Morty and Dov, our friends who work there. Another round of drinks and embraces and crazy dances while we waited for the historic First Edition to come off the presses. At 4:30 in the morning, flushed with excitement, ignoring the wet ink, we passed our copies around for everyone to autograph, including an English Tommy [soldier] who wandered in for a drink. Then Morty, Dov, Milt and Ray Sussman, and I and several student friends who had come with me headed back to the Sochnut building, just in time to see a streak of warm beauty spring up out of the horizon and smile good morning to us. We looked at each other, drew closer together, wrapped arms about each other's chilled shoulders and felt the thrill of experiencing a historic wonder, dawn bidding Shalom [peace] to a Jewish State.

Our group consisted of about fourteen fellows and a few girls, from about as many countries. We made our way singing to Morty's room, not far away, where we found the landlord so elated he didn't know what to do for us first. Ever the practical person, I suggested food and prepared sandwiches, fruit and coffee while we drank yet another "*Le Chaim*" [toast to life]. Leaving the house, we were met by scores of morning crowds, some from the night before, some fresh out of bed, kissing and embracing and shouting "Mazal tov!" And as we rounded the corner into Keren Kayemet Street, where the Sochnut is, whiz came the motorcycles, lorries [trucks], cars and the children, now awake, and took up the gaiety where we had left off. Spontaneous parades formed, led by a flag bearer and a couple of drunken British soldiers—this time, thank goodness, unarmed.

> "
> Ben-Gurion tossed his head back proudly . . . and charged the air with electricity when he shouted defiantly, 'WE ARE A FREE PEOPLE.'
> "

The sun was getting warmer and warmer, a glorious day. The end of November, and seventy-five degrees of heartwarming sunshine was bearing down on a happy city. The foreign correspondents and Pathé [newsreel] men were on the job photographing the British tanks which were suddenly converted into flying transport for anyone who could climb aboard, sing, shout and wave a flag. We joined the crowds, going from one end of King George V Street to the other, meeting friends and fraternizing with the English soldiers, who were as happy as we were about the end of tension and ill feeling between us. All they wanted was to go home. With each round we ended up at the Sochnut again; every crowd did.

Long Live the Jewish State!

Rumor had it that [David] Ben-Gurion [chairman of the Jewish Agency] had just arrived from Tel Aviv and would make a personal appearance. Sure enough, there he was, standing on the balcony of the Sochnut building. He looked slowly and solemnly around him—to the roof tops crammed with people, to the throngs that stood solid in the courtyard below him. He raised his hand: an utter silence waited for his words. "*Ashreynu shezachinu layom hazeh.*" (Blessed are we who have been privileged to witness this day.) He concluded with "*Techi Hamedinah*

Ha'ivrit" (Long Live the Hebrew State—it didn't have a name yet) and called for *Hatikvah*. A solemn chant rose from all sides. The moment was too big for our feelings. There were few dry eyes and few steady voices. Ben-Gurion tossed his head back proudly, tenderly touched the flag that hung from the railing and charged the air with electricity when he shouted defiantly, "WE ARE A FREE PEOPLE."

How I wished you could have heard his words and been here for this memorable night and never-to-be-forgotten morning. It was too unbelievable.

Making my way to the bus to go home for a camera and a wash, I noticed that all the cafes and wine shops had flung open their doors—drinks on the house. Flags were hoisted everywhere and shopkeepers had decorated their windows with photos of Theodor Herzl [founder of the Zionist political movement], whose words have inspired and sustained Zionists until this day: "If you will it, it is no dream." Now that it was happening, it seemed more than ever like a dream. My heart was bursting from joy.

Later that night . . .
I grabbed my camera, changed clothes and joined my friends to return to the city and the excitement. Notices were already prominently displayed announcing a mass meeting to be held in the Sochnut courtyard at 3:00 in the afternoon, and a very impressive affair it was. We had already heard that there were incidents of Arab ambushes on the road from Haifa to Jerusalem. The crowds were more sober and, when told to, dispersed in an orderly and disciplined manner, everyone going to his own home and his own family celebration. We had ours too, then a hot bath and off to sleep, trying to make up for about fifty non-stop hours of delirium.

Your loving daughter,
Zippy

A Young Immigrant
Joins the Haganah

David Rubinger, with Ruth Corman

In the following viewpoint, David Rubinger describes his experiences in Israel in 1947 and 1948 during the days immediately preceding and following the Israeli declaration of independence. He tells how he and his neighbors and others in the city of Jerusalem reacted to the news that a majority vote was cast for the establishment of a Jewish state in Palestine. He goes on to describe his induction into the Jewish defense organization, the Haganah, and his battlefront experiences in the fight against Arab invaders. Rubinger and Ruth Corman are co-authors of *Israel Through My Lens*, from which this viewpoint is excerpted. Rubinger, who was born in Vienna and immigrated to Israel in 1939, is a photojournalist acknowledged internationally for his photographs depicting the history of Israel. Corman is a London-based photographer, art consultant, and curator of the British Israel Arts Foundation.

Anni and I started married life living in one room in Jerusalem. We had absolutely nothing except a camp bed provided by the Jewish Agency. We found bricks and a plank to make a bookcase and managed to acquire two secondhand armchairs, which, we acknowledged, gave a real air of luxury to our surroundings. Suddenly I found myself, aged twenty-two, living in Palestine with a now-pregnant wife—two and a half of us in one extremely small room. . . .

Anni had a part-time job cleaning houses, and for the first time I sold some of my photographs—to neighbors, for six piastres [the currency of the Ottoman Empire] apiece. I think that it was not so much the money, which was a very small amount, but rather the satisfaction of knowing that someone placed such value on my pictures that they were prepared to part with real currency to possess them!

A Vote for Partition

One of the very earliest photographs I took was an image of some of my neighbors thrusting bread through a barbed wire fence to their relatives and friends. This took place during one of the many curfews imposed by the British in certain areas of Jerusalem. Roads were cut off from each other with barbed wire, largely in response to the activities of the Jewish terrorist group, the Irgun, who were proving troublesome and outright dangerous to the British authorities.

> It was no time for dancing and singing as we had a dangerous road ahead.

On November 18, 1947, our first child, a daughter we named Tami, was born. The atmosphere in Palestine was very tense because of the ongoing UN deliberations as to the future of the country. There were frequent attacks by local Arabs, and it had become so dangerous that when it came time to deliver Tami, Anni had to be escorted up to the hospital on Mount Scopus in a British armored car.

Eleven days later, on November 29, towards midnight, the United Nations voted for the partition of Palestine into a Jewish and an Arab state. For anyone privileged to have been living there at the time, this surely was one of the most momentous happenings that one could have imagined. We, along with all our neighbors, were glued to the radio. At midnight, a majority vote was cast for the establishment of a Jewish state in Palestine. The city erupted with milling crowds thronging the streets, singing, dancing, and celebrating. Anni went out to buy cigarettes from a nearby kiosk. The kiosk owner gave her the cigarettes but refused payment. "Tonight," he said, "I am not accepting any money from anyone."

A photograph by David Rubinger shows barricaded members of the Jewish Agency's Haganah defense division in Jerusalem. **(David Rubinger/Time & Life Pictures/Getty Images.)**

From Celebration to Danger

The celebrations continued all night and well into the next day. It was on the morning of this day that I took

> Seven countries joined in the jihad, with five of them, Saudi Arabia, Transjordan, Lebanon, Egypt, and Iraq, deciding to invade our newly formed state of Israel.

one of my most arresting images, that of a British armored car in the center of Jerusalem onto which ten or more young children and teenagers had scrambled, waving handmade Jewish flags, laughing, and cheering. . . .

On that same day in 1947, David Ben-Gurion, with great prescience, warned that it was no time for dancing and singing as we had a dangerous road ahead of us. He could not have been more right, and in fact it was only one day later, on December 1, that I took pictures of Arab rioters burning Jewish shops in the commercial center then located behind the King David Hotel.

I also shot pictures of our unofficial army, the Haganah, who were attempting to reach the area in trucks but were prevented from doing so by British armored cars, which had blocked the streets. . . .

The Haganah and Independence

The Haganah had been formed in 1920 as a clandestine force for Jewish self-defense. Originally composed of individual units active in different towns and settlements throughout Palestine, the Haganah gradually grew into the central defense mechanism of the Zionist movement. After the State of Israel was declared, the Haganah became the Israel Defense Forces.

In mid-December 1947, I was inducted into the Haganah and sent up to Mount Scopus for training. This activity was then considered illegal and had to be covert, as the British still controlled the country. We had a gun or two, but mostly we used make-believe guns made out of sticks.

Those of my contemporaries and I who had received military training from the British Army (about five thousand soldiers) were part of the nucleus, together with the Haganah, that eventually became Israel's legitimate army. Our experience proved invaluable; indeed, my second lieutenant in the British Army went on to become a major general in the Israeli army many years later.

The British decided to relinquish the responsibilities of the Mandate, given to them in 1919, on May 14, 1948. This thereafter became the official Independence Day of Israel, the historic occasion when David Ben-Gurion declared the establishment of the State of Israel upon the departure of the British troops.

Serious fighting began immediately the next day, with the Muslims declaring a *jihad* (holy war) on the fledgling state. Their intentions were made clear by Azzam Pasha, Secretary-General of the Arab League, when he declared, "This will be a war of extermination and a momentous massacre which will be spoken of like the Mongolian massacres and the Crusades."

Defending Against Arab Invasion

Seven countries joined in the jihad, with five of them, Saudi Arabia, Transjordan, Lebanon, Egypt, and Iraq, deciding to invade our newly formed State of Israel. They were well armed and equipped, in great contrast to the makeshift weaponry that we had at our disposal.

That same day, May 15, proved to be one of the most unforgettable days of my life. My military group, dressed in civilian clothes, had taken up positions on Jaffa Road, Jerusalem, in a building that housed Barclays Bank and later became the municipal offices of the city. The building faced the Jaffa Gate of the Old City, next to which was David's Tower—a tall edifice with a commanding view of the whole area.

> I remember crouching, huddled down behind the wall, looking at a nearby tree as bullets tore into its trunk and branches.

Among our inadequate weaponry, we had just one homemade two-inch mortar and two cases of shells.

What we failed to realize, however, was that the shells we had were a fraction of a millimeter larger than the barrel of the mortar, so it was impossible to use them without first filing down the fins of the shells to reduce their size.

I was the one "volunteered" to return to our HQ [headquarters], . . . to try to find a file. This I managed to do, but on returning I did not know that the building immediately on the left of our previous position was now occupied by Arab snipers. It did not take long for me to realize what had happened, as the whole area, including the little garden that I had to traverse to get back, was being liberally peppered with gunshot.

I took shelter behind a low wall about twenty inches high, alongside two other Haganah fighters. They were both killed. I survived. I remember crouching, huddled down behind the wall, looking at a nearby tree as bullets tore into its trunk and branches. I went back to visit this tree many years later and could still see signs of the wounds it had suffered that day.

I lay there for some time, perhaps twenty meters from the safety of our post, when suddenly an armored car . . . which the Haganah had presumably "requisitioned" from the British, came into view. A man in the vehicle motioned for me to make a dash for it while its occupants poured heavy fire onto the enemy positions. I did as he suggested, armed solely with my file for protection. I got back. . . .

A Fight for Survival

Two of the places where I was involved in the street fighting were Yemin Moshe and Mount Zion. Both of these areas were extremely vulnerable as they were totally exposed to fire from the Jordanian positions on the top of the Old City walls. One of the earliest photographs I have of myself in this war shows me crouching behind a stone wall, wearing a sports jacket and clutching a Sten gun [submachine gun] in Yemin Moshe. Today this place is the location of Mishkenot Sha'ananim, a very elegant residence where visiting artists from around the world are invited to stay. Quite a contrast to how it was when I was there trying to defend it!

After surviving these episodes, I was sent on an officers' training course by the then-established Israeli army, although we were still in makeshift uniforms and without insignia. I became a platoon commander, the equivalent of a second lieutenant.

We soon found ourselves once again stationed in a building opposite the Tower of David. The Tower was under the control of the Arab Legion. Their arsenal included a six-pound gun with which they continually bombarded our position. I remember that the shells went in one side and came straight out of the other side of the building. On one occasion, I needed to go downstairs to check on a machine gun. When I returned upstairs, the place where I had slept and where my desk and phone had been had simply disappeared. Someone somewhere must have been watching out for me again!

Israel won the War of Independence against overwhelming odds, but the Tower of David remained in the hands of the Jordanian army for the next nineteen years, until 1967, when Israel again took control of the Old City.

A Diplomat Begins His Mission in Israel

James G. McDonald

In the following viewpoint, James G. McDonald relates what went on during his first four days as the first U.S. ambassador to Israel. He describes his arrival in 1948, including the changes he observes on the drive to Tel Aviv, and talks about conditions in Tel Aviv and how the city and its inhabitants have been affected by the flood of Jewish refugees and resulting conflict with the Arab population. He goes on to describe his meeting with the Israeli foreign minister and his visit with prime minister David Ben-Gurion and his wife at their home. James G. McDonald was the American ambassador to Israel from 1948 to 1951. Prior to that he served in many other official capacities, including chairman of the Foreign Policy Association, High Commissioner for Refugees Coming from Germany, chairman of the President's Advisory Committee on Political Refugees, and member of the Anglo-American Committee of Inquiry on Palestine.

SOURCE. James G. McDonald, *My Mission in Israel 1948–1951.* New York: Simon & Schuster, 1951. Copyright © 1951 by James G. McDonald. Copyright © renewed 1979 by Mrs. James G. McDonald. Reproduced by permission of Simon & Schuster, Inc.

After a brief stop in Athens [Greece], we made an auspicious arrival in midafternoon, August 12th, at the Haifa Airport in Israel.

We were greeted by officials of the Israel Government and a military guard of honor, and members of our own staffs at Haifa and Tel Aviv, headed by our Counselor, Charles Knox, who had left Washington a few weeks before me. We underwent the barrage of newspaper and motion picture photographers with such grace as we could muster, and with what we hoped would later appear as appropriate casualness. The trip down the heavily traveled coastal road to Tel Aviv, a distance of about sixty-five miles along the Mediterranean, took more than two hours despite an escort of police motorcycles and a military car with plain-clothes officers. How different this ride from my earlier journey along this same ancient road, for millennia the route of imperial conquerors! In 1946 and 1947 the road had been jammed with British military convoys, heavy equipment, racing military police cars and motorcycles, with road-blocks every few miles and constant interrogation by the British military. Now there were no British. Arabs with their picturesque donkeys and camels were no more. Bombed-out, razed Arab and Jewish villages, and neglected orange groves were mute witnesses of recent fighting. Everywhere Jews were working with pick and shovel, tractors and bulldozers.

> " There was a press interview during which I stressed . . . that I felt as if I had come 'home.' "

Arrival in Tel Aviv

Within Tel Aviv one of the main streets had been cleared. We drove quickly to our abode, the Gat Rimmon, one of a series of small hotels which front on Hayarkon Street, running parallel to the sea, and which boast teatime and restaurant terraces looking out on the Mediterranean.

The reception from the public was enthusiastic. We were flattered by the press estimates of thousands waiting to cheer us. Again and again [my daughter] Bobby and I had to face the cameras. There was a press interview during which I stressed . . . that I felt as if I had come "home." This, judging from the press reactions, was a fortunate phrase; it had the advantage, too, of being sincere.

Finally, we were allowed to go up to our rooms. Knox had held out to us the prospect of the best rooms in the hotel; he had kept his promise! My tiny room duly looked out on the Mediterranean; Bobby and [my secretary] Miss [Harriet] Clark shared a room barely big enough for two cots and a washstand. Between the two rooms was a bath but no toilet.

Our quarters were wide open to curious eyes or ears—friendly or otherwise; we developed a goldfish complex [from living visible to all, as a goldfish in a bowl]. In the interests perhaps of cleanliness, the bathroom was the one secluded spot. Immediately below us was the outdoor café where every day except Shabat [Jewish Sabbath] a dance orchestra played with enthusiastic use of brass until midnight. Last of all there was no telephone in our rooms.

> Rationing was already under way, meat was in short supply and good coffee was already a luxury.

The Reality of Life in Tel Aviv

Why should we have been so inadequately housed? The answer is that Jerusalem, not Tel Aviv, had been the prewar tourist center. Now the town was terribly overcrowded because of the war and the uneasy truce which had brought with it a crowd of UN observers who completely filled one of the best hotels. Our hotel was particularly crowded because it was also playing host to the members of the Russian delegation, who had arrived only three days before us. . . .

At my first dinner at the Gat we were waited on as if we were royalty, but the food was indifferent: frozen fish, eggplant and potatoes, no meat, butter or milk, insipid dessert and worse coffee. Nonetheless we knew that it was far better than that received by the Israel citizenry. Rationing was already under way, meat was in short supply and good coffee was already a luxury. A number of factors lay behind this. A goodly percentage of Israeli manpower—and woman power—was still under arms, and the best of what food there was went to them. At the same time the tidal flood of ingathering Jewish refugees (they were then arriving at the rate of seventeen thousand a month, a figure soon to reach as high as thirty thousand) was beginning to make more and more demands upon Israel's inadequate larder. As rationing tightened, food in public places and in private homes (other than those of diplomats) became less and less varied. Meat, butter and even potatoes became nearly unobtainable; but miraculously, no one seemed to be undernourished. Fish substituted for meat; an excellent local margarine for butter; eggplant and Brussels sprouts for other vegetables; and plentiful citrus fruits or juices for other desserts. Eggs and milk were reserved primarily for invalids and children. The latter could not have been huskier.

A Truce Not Honored

Feeling a desperate need to get away from the noise and eyes of the hotel—I had trouble sleeping—Bobby and I sought refuge at [president of the Women's International Zionist Organization] Rebecca Sieff's beautiful estate at Tel Mond, about forty miles from Tel Aviv.

> The next day came new evidence of a truce that was honored more in the breach than in the observance.

We were seated on the veranda there when we heard rifle shots. [Security officer Eugene F.] McMahon immediately ordered us inside, and investigated. He returned to announce, "Truce or no truce, at this moment the Iraqi troops are stationed only about four or five miles from here, and those rifle shots came from their direction. I'm afraid we'll have to consider Tel Mond out of bounds."

Reluctantly we returned to the Gat Rimmon and its blaring dance music. My staff continued their search to find permanent headquarters for us that would be practical in terms of both diplomatic needs and security.

The next day came new evidence of a truce that was honored more in the breach than in the observance. Word came that the Arabs had blown up the Jerusalem water-pumping station at Latrun. Jerusalem then received its water from natural springs near Petah Tikva, about twenty miles from the coast, and Latrun was the point at which the pipelines carrying the water began their climb up the Judean hills to Jerusalem. The fact that the pumps were under the protection of UN guards made the truce violation a particularly flagrant one. And it underlined more clearly than the Iraqi sniping how powerful a blow could be struck by one side against the other even while a "truce" was in force.

> The next day—four days after our arrival in Israel—the Prime Minister, disregarding protocol, invited . . . me to his house for an informal visit.

Meeting with the Foreign Minister

In this atmosphere I began my round of official calls. My first was upon the Foreign Minister, Moshe Sharett, at his office in Sarona, the former German Templar suburb of Tel Aviv. He was then Moshe Shertok, but later, in line with the desire of the Prime Minister, supported by strong public opinion, he Hebraized his name, as did scores of other Israel officials. Sarona was an excellent choice as a governmental headquarters. Wisely, the Provisional Government, instead of requisitioning one of the better sections of Tel Aviv, had taken over this suburb, which for some years had been used by the British Army and police, and left almost a total wreck when the British withdrew from Palestine. Now it was being rapidly rebuilt into an attractive and convenient government center, called Hakirya—Hebrew for "The Town." Despite the heat of the day, Sharett's office and balcony overlooking a little garden were pleasantly cool.

The Foreign Minister, in his early fifties—dark, intelligent, enormously erudite and energetic—greeted me warmly. . . . As befitted a first meeting, the rest of our talk was general. Sharett did, however, tell me that elections for Israel's first Constituent Assembly would probably be held in September and a constitutional regime established as soon as possible thereafter.

My second call was on Mrs. Golda Myerson [later Meir], soon to leave as Israel's first Minister to Moscow, and later to be Minister of Labor. . . .

A Visit with the Prime Minister

The next day—four days after our arrival in Israel—the Prime Minister [David Ben-Gurion], disregarding protocol, invited Bobby and me to his house for an informal visit. Knox went along. Ben-Gurion and his very devoted, energetic and unconventional wife, Paula, lived very modestly in a small, unmodern and simply furnished house. Its simplicity was relieved by Ben-Gurion's fine library, one of the best private collections in the Middle East, which occupied most of the upper floor.

The Ben-Gurions received us like old friends. B.G.—as he is known to everyone in the Government—was as I had last seen him when he testified before our Committee in Jerusalem in early 1946—the same stocky figure, with the same shock of white hair rising in an undisciplined fringe around his head, and the same piercing but friendly look in his blue eyes. He rose from a chair in the living room and, shaking hands warmly, made me at once feel at home. I had known him for several years and had often discussed Palestine and Jewish problems with him. Indeed, when our Committee was hearing testimony in Jerusalem, one of my British colleagues on the Committee took advantage of our known friendship to pay me a dubious compliment. According to the wholly false rumor which he had spread, I "had given Ben-Gurion instructions" the night before he was to testify as to the relations between the Jewish Agency, of which he was then the head, and the Jewish underground army, the Haganah!

A Tea Time Air Raid

While we were having tea in the tiny living room, there was a sudden shrill scream of a siren. "It's an air raid," Paula Ben-Gurion announced, and before it had stopped, she insisted that her husband follow his own regulations. We all trooped into an improvised air-raid shelter used by the Prime Minister—the next-door room with a reinforced ceiling. Ben-Gurion gave the planes one contemptuous sentence: "They come from the Egyptian lines about thirty-five miles south of here."

With that announcement, we continued our talk, maintaining the pretense that nothing was happening outside.

One peculiarity of the air-raid warnings in Israel led to endless arguments in our household and, I suppose, in many others. Because of the short distance the Egyptian planes had to fly—usually less than ten minutes' flying time—at times we heard the thuds of the bombs before the sirens sounded. Then would ensue the argument: Was the raid over or not? Was it worth while to leave lunch or dinner, or get up out of a warm bed, to go to a so-called shelter? (In the residence we obtained shortly after we arrived, we were supposed to go to the basement.) Gradually, as the raids continued over the course of months, we went less and less to the shelters, becoming, we liked to pretend, fatalists.

A Palestinian Arab Remembers the 1948 Arab-Israeli War

Ilene R. Prusher

In the following viewpoint, Ilene R. Prusher focuses on the recollections and views of an elderly Palestinian, Mahmoud Jadallah, who lived and fought in Palestine against the Israelis in 1947 and during the 1948 Arab-Israeli War. He still lives in the same area he did then, but it no longer is Arab land; it was annexed by Israel after the 1967 Six-Day War. Jadallah describes his war experiences and relates how important his land was—and still is—to him and his family. He expresses his sentiments about partition and shares his frustrations with the British for favoring the Zionists, with the surrounding Arab countries for not providing enough aid when it was needed, and with the lack of Arab unity both in the past and in the present. Ilene R. Prusher is a staff writer for the *Christian Science Monitor*.

Mahmoud Jadallah recalls the 1948 Arab-Israeli war as if it were yesterday. As he guides a visitor through the village he once defended against Israeli forces, the names of outposts and passwords his Arab fighters used trip off his tongue.

But the day that the Jordanians told them to stop fighting is clearest. The war was over—for the moment, at least—and an armistice had been reached between Israel and Jordan. "The Jordanians came along with us and said, 'OK, we don't need you anymore. You can go home. We're in charge now. They're a state, and we're a state.'

"One of our soldiers couldn't believe what had happened. In front of everyone, he put his rifle under his feet and broke it, destroyed it. He said, 'Losing the soil of this land, which is mixed with our blood, this is something I cannot take,'" Mr. Jadallah recalls.

Frustrations

A Jordanian officer chastised the soldier. "This weapon you broke, you should have sold it to buy food for your family." After that, says Jadallah, no one said a word, and the only sounds were of people crying.

While Israelis kicked off the 60th anniversary of their independence [on May 8, 2008,] in celebrations that are expected to continue in the coming weeks, Palestinians are beginning to mark the same series of events as the *nakba*, or catastrophe.

Just south of Sur Baher, the former Arab village south of Jerusalem where Jadallah fought, young Palestinian demonstrators in Bethlehem carried an enormous key through town [on May 8] as a symbol of their longing to return to homes they—or more specifically, their parents and grandparents—lost in 1948. But it is the older generation

> '[The Israeli takeover] was like an earthquake that falls upon people and shakes them up. After it's over, people start looking around for what's left.'

of Palestinians who most intimately knows the details of the sea-change they lived through 60 years ago, and who have the most telling tales to share. And many, like Jadallah, feel almost as frustrated with the state of today's political realities—especially the searing split within Palestinian society between the West Bank and the Gaza Strip—as they did six decades ago.

"It was like an earthquake that falls upon people and shakes them up. After it's over, people start looking around for what's left," Jadallah explains, looking out from his balcony toward the semiarid mountains leading out to the desert to the places where he's seen many an army pass: from the British to the Jordanians to the Israelis.

With Jerusalem visible in the background, several Arab gunmen pose in a foxhole from which they attack Jewish buses traveling to and from the city in 1948. (©Bettmann/Corbis.)

A Shared Blame

In 1947, Jadallah was sent to Syria by Abdel Qader Husseini, a military leader of the Arab forces in what was British-controlled Mandatory Palestine, for training.

"It was known that the British were going to withdraw, and that's why we were planning to have an army. The idea was for us to go to Syria and come back able to train others," he explains.

Things did not go the way they planned, and for this, he points the blame in many directions. He lays it at the feet of the British, which he believes made it easy for Zionist militias to gain the upper hand: a photographic negative of the historical picture seen by most Israelis.

But he also blames the surrounding Arab countries for not providing enough aid. His strongest memories are of "irregulars" from places as far off as Yemen, and a contingent from the Muslim Brotherhood in Egypt.

"We were shocked to see that the British withdrawal did not equal our ascendancy. They gave all of their sites and locations and equipment to the Jews," Jadallah says. "Our capacity was very weak. We didn't have the same weaponry they did. We only had some simple rifles and ammunition."

Sur Baher wasn't a particularly wealthy area, and Jadallah remembers people scrambling for enough money to buy weapons. "We were 105 men in this village and we relied on our own personal resources," he says. "Anyone who had a wife who had a bracelet or necklace asked her to sell it so we could buy guns. We armed ourselves from our own personal resources. But we were starting to see that the British withdrawal was facilitating the coming of the Jewish state."

> 'Our only option was to protect the land on which we were living, because we saw that the Jews were taking much more than the partition called for.'

A Need for Arab Unity

In retrospect, he says he regrets that the Partition Plan for Palestine, passed by the fledgling United Nations on Nov. 29, 1947, was a failure. Palestinian Arabs felt they had no choice but to fight it, he says, because they didn't feel the division of land was fair. Israel agreed to the partition plan and Arab states rejected it, which led to the outbreak of the war and Israel's declaration of statehood less than six months later.

"We liked the concept of partition, but we felt it was not done correctly," Jadallah sighs. "We reached a moment where partition was an opportunity, and we missed it. Our only option was to protect the land on which we were living, because we saw that the Jews were taking much more than the partition called for." Israel's portion of the land in the partition plan was indeed designated to be smaller than what it became by mid-1948; Zionist leaders believed the partition's narrow borders to be indefensible.

Jadallah says he wishes that Arabs would have been more united in their stance and strategy. He looks at the splits then—those who favored a cease-fire and those who didn't—and can't help but look with dismay at the schism in Palestinian society now, following [militant Islamic group] Hamas's takeover of Gaza [in 2007]. Gaza, where many Palestinian refugees fled to in 1948, is now cut off from the Palestine Liberation Organization–run Palestinian Authority in the West Bank.

"We weren't united then and we're not now," he says, sitting in the reception room, in which he has pictures of Jerusalem and a photograph of him embracing Yasser Arafat, the Palestinian leader whom he outlived. In Jadallah's eyes, no one will again be able to bring together Palestinians the way Arafat did. At the same time, he adds, "Arafat was never satisfied with what he was being given, so he got nothing.

"Had all Arabs been united in 1948, we would really have created an impact. Israel was so tiny then and we were big," he says. "Today, it's essentially the same. We are as disunited now as we were in 1948."

> 'All of this makes me sad . . . because it makes me feel like we didn't achieve anything.'

A Village Transformed

Sur Baher remained part of Jordan until the Six-Day War of 1967, when Israel occupied the West Bank. Israel later annexed Sur Baher and other Arab neighborhoods and villages to Jerusalem, expanding the city boundaries several times, and thousands of East Jerusalemites like Jadallah were given Israeli IDs with the status of "permanent resident."

Sixty years on, they're still not citizens of any country. They can, however, get rights afforded to Israeli citizens, such as education and healthcare, and travel on Jordanian or Palestinian passports.

And so in an area that Israel counts as part of its capital, Jadallah can still, in a short walk from his home, visit the very sites where he once fought.

First he passes the school that his men used as a base, which is, once again, a school. Then he goes by a hill where some of the heaviest fighting took place, where there were casualties on both sides.

"This was one of the trenches," he says, pointing to a hidden cement box embedded in the hillside, with two holes through which guards would watch or shoot. "It was called 'mujahid,'" Arabic for one who wages holy war. "You can see how crucial this one was, because all of the Jewish settlements nearby were exposed to it. Every night, I would come and supervise the trenches. There was a password for anyone who came near."

They changed it all the time, but it always started with a hard Arabic "h"—one that they could count on most of their enemies to mispronounce because Hebrew has a different, more guttural "h."

"The years of 1948 to 1950 were years of sacrifice. We lost a lot of colleagues, of homes, of land. All of this makes me sad," he says, "because it makes me feel like we didn't achieve anything."

Living with the Reality

Jadallah went on to have a large family—seven girls and three boys—and now has close to 70 grandchildren and great-grandchildren.

To many of them, living with Israel is a reality with which they grew up. Jadallah's son, Nihad, has worked with Israel's ambulance service, Magen David Adom, for 27 years. He speaks excellent Hebrew and is clean-shaven. Still, Nihad says he feels there's still great discrimination in how he's treated at work.

Not long ago, he says, when his father was [not] feeling well, he couldn't get his own ambulance company to enter Sur Baher without an Israeli army escort, causing a half-hour delay. He still feels suspect, the "other." He is expected to come to an Israeli Independence day celebration for all employees and was struggling with whether to go. But earlier this week, when colleagues at work were receiving free Israeli flags to put on their cars, he drew the line. "It's not my flag," he says, "and it's not my state."

A Jewish-American Teen Personally Encounters the Arab-Israeli Conflict

Rachel Sacks

In the following viewpoint, Rachel Sacks describes her emotions during a visit to Israel as a participant in Young Judea's Machon program. She explains how, never before having met any Palestinian Arabs or heard their stories firsthand, the visit proved a great revelation. She tells how moved she was by a young Arab-Christian woman, a speaker for a coexistence group, who shared her experiences and expressed her anti-Jewish sentiments. Sacks tells how difficult it was for her to listen to the young woman and explains why she felt listening was something she had to do. She goes on to acknowledge that the woman's bitterness was justified and tells how the woman's words brought home to her the depth of the hostility felt by Arabs toward Israel. Rachel Sacks was a high school senior in Milburn, New Jersey, at the time this was written.

SOURCE. Rachel Sacks, "Close Encounters with the Arab-Israeli Conflict," *JVibe*, October 2007. Copyright © 2007 JVibe. JVibe is the Web site and national magazine for Jewish teens. Reproduced by permission.

When I packed my two very large suitcases for my trip to Israel with Young Judaea's Machon program, I did not prepare for the reality of the country. Machon is a five-and-a-half week trip that starts in the Negev [desert in southern Israel] and moves North, allowing teens to experience an off-the-beaten-track view of Israel.

I had not prepared myself for what I was presented with on Machon: the extensive poverty, the tension between secular and religious Jews (like two different worlds), the immigrant disparity—how Russians and Ethiopians struggle to assimilate into Israeli society. Most of all, I did not prepare myself for my own intimate encounter with the Palestinian conflict.

> " Hearing Sorayda's story was the hardest and truest experience of my time in Israel. "

Though I had learned about the conflict at camp, Hebrew school, youth group and high school, never had I confronted the complex tension between Arabs and Jews face-to-face. Never had I met a Palestinian or an Arab-Israeli myself, nor heard his or her story. Thus, hearing Sorayda's story was the hardest and truest experience of my time in Israel.

Sorayda's Story

Sorayda was young and pretty, her hair pulled back, her clothes modern. She wore tight pants, high heels and a tank top. She visited us in Nazareth, at the inn that her family owned. A young mother, Sorayda represented the Arab-Christian minority in Nazareth, as indicated by her Western clothing. She came to us as a speaker for a coexistence group, ready to share her perspective with a group of Zionist, American teenagers. None of us expected her to say what she did; she was, after all, with a coexistence group, dressed as an American might [be], speaking to Jews—what could she say that would shock us?

She spoke casually, joking about her shoes, mentioning her Jewish best friends. As she warmed up, however, she began to speak of her intrinsic distrust for Jews, a deep loathing in her heart. She did not identify Israel as her home, but Nazareth as her home; she viewed Israel with contempt and identified herself as an Arab first. She talked about her grandpa—how his land was taken in the 1967 war, and how Jewish soldiers came to his property and beat him when he returned to pick some olives.

Sorayda talked about how Jews dominate the American government, how they are rich and greedy and want to own everything—rattling off stereotypes one after another, much to everyone's dismay. She scornfully referred to the "Israeli mentality," how Jews take everything, stuffing their pockets.

> Sorayda represented an inkling of the conflict; she was the conflict, adorned in Western garb and a sweet smile.

And then she mentioned how she likes France because Jews are treated with suspicion there, and Arabs are treated better. She described watching "that Jew guy," as she called him, searched at the French airport, and the pleasure she obtained from the experience.

She was bitter, her views extreme for an Arab Christian, more akin to those of an Arab Muslim. My friends looked outraged as we sat through her speech, feeling uncomfortable, attacked.

Yet, while I did not want to hear what Sorayda had to say, I knew I had to; I knew that listening to her was a valuable experience, and as hard as it was to admit, I understood her cynicism. Her experiences had produced such resentment. What mother wants her child to grow up feeling inferior? She mentioned how becoming a mother had hardened her perspective, how she cringed to think her son would have to feel as small as she had. She told us how her son, only 6 1/2, played with a Jewish girl next door, his best friend, but one day the girl told him he should take care; he was Arab. How can one blame her for her hostility?

Bridging the Gap

While Sorayda harbored so much contempt, I kept in mind that she was speaking for coexistence, however ironic it seemed. For all her stereotypes and virulent views, she was making a deliberate effort to bridge relations between Jews and Arabs. She emphasized that we were all human beings, and she wished for no religion to divide people.

As other kids exchanged angry glances and whispers, I tried to respect her views, to understand them, to absorb the experience. This hostility, in so much conflict with my own views, was very real and represented just a drop of the hostility felt toward Israel.

Even more so, her bitterness was justified. In Israeli society, Arabs are constantly treated as inferior—even Arab-Israeli citizens and Arab Christians like her, although with less enmity than Arab Muslims. Sorayda represented an inkling of the conflict; she was the conflict, adorned in Western garb and a sweet smile.

Always hospitable, our kind Arab hosts served us black Arabic coffee at the end of the seminar—bitter, like the views on both sides.

GLOSSARY

Aliyah Large-scale immigration of Jews to Israel or the Holy Land (plural: aliyot).

Arab League Coalition of Arab states founded in 1945 to strengthen and coordinate political, cultural, economic, and social programs and to mediate disputes.

Balfour Declaration Statement named for Lord Balfour issued by the British in 1917 recognizing the right of the Jewish people to establish a national home in Palestine with consideration for the rights of non-Jewish Palestinians.

diaspora A population dispersed from its settled territory; can refer to both Palestinians living in areas other than the West Bank, Gaza, and Israel and Jews living outside of Palestine or present-day Israel.

Eretz Yisrael Land of Israel; the homeland promised to the Israelites in the Bible.

Haganah Jewish defense organization that operated underground during the British Mandate and, after the creation of Israel in 1948, became the core of the Israel Defense Forces.

Hatikvah "The Hope"; the national anthem of Israel.

Holocaust The systematic killing of approximately six million Jews by the Nazis and their collaborators from the 1930s to the end of World War II.

Intifada Armed uprising of the Palestinians that began in December of 1987 to protest Israeli policies and occupation of the West Bank and Gaza Strip.

Irgun Underground Jewish terrorist organization very active during

198

and after World War II in operations against British authorities in Palestine and against Arab civilians.

iron wall — Term created in 1923 by Zionist leader Vladimir (Ze'ev) Jabotinsky to express his contention that the Jews would have to deal with the Arabs from a position of great strength if they ever wanted to be able to negotiate a reasonable peace with them.

Jewish Agency — Group established originally under the terms of the British Mandate to promote Jewish immigration and to administer the affairs of the Jewish community in Palestine prior to the 1948 declaration of the state of Israel.

jihad — Islamic holy war waged against non-Muslims.

kibbutz — Israeli collective farm or settlement.

Lovers of Zion — Organizations established in the early 1800s to promote Jewish settlement, mostly agricultural, in Israel.

mandate — Authority granted to a state by the League of Nations to govern a particular region in order to promote self-government.

Medinat Yisrael — The State of Israel.

mujahid — Muslim who takes part in a holy war.

Nakba — Arabic term meaning "catastrophe" used by Palestinians for the flight and expulsion of Palestinian Arabs in 1948 and the defeat of the Arab armies in the 1948 Arab-Israeli War.

Olim — Persons who immigrate to Israel.

Palmach — Jewish military force in Palestine created with British cooperation in 1941 that became the Haganah's leading commando force.

right of return — Moral and legal right of Arab refugees and their descendents to return to their pre-1948 homes in Israel and the occupied territories.

Stern Gang	Jewish terrorist group created in 1939 and disbanded in 1948; also known as Fighters for Israel's Freedom.
War of Independence	Term used by Jews and Israelis to refer to the first war (November 1947–March 1949) between the state of Israel and neighboring Arab countries.
White Paper	Document issued in 1939 that defined British policy regarding Palestine, closing Palestine to any further Jewish immigration.
Yishuv	The Jewish community in Palestine before Israel was declared a state in 1948.
Zionism	Political movement founded as an official organization in 1897 by Jewish journalist Theodor Herzl for the return of the Jewish people to their homeland and the establishment of a Jewish state in Palestine.

CHRONOLOGY

1882	The First Aliyah (large-scale immigration of Jews to Israel) begins, consisting mostly of Jews from eastern Europe.
1896	Austrian journalist Theodore Herzl publishes Der Judenstaat ("The Jewish State"), a pamphlet arguing for a Jewish state.
1897	The First Jewish Zionist Congress convenes in Basel, Switzerland; the World Zionist Organization is founded.
1903	The First Aliyah ends.
1904	The Second Aliyah begins, consisting mostly of Jews from Russia and Poland.
1909	The first modern all-Jewish city, Tel Aviv, is founded.
1910	The first kibbutz (collective farm), Degania Aleph, is founded.
1913	The Second Aliyah ends.
1914	World War I begins.
1916	The Arabs revolt against Turkish Ottoman rule; the Sykes-Picot Agreement divides the Middle East into areas of influence for France, Great Britain, and others.
1917	The British government issues the Balfour Declaration,

pledging support for establishment of a "Jewish national home" in Palestine.

1918 World War I ends; the British bring to an end four hundred years of Ottoman rule in Palestine.

1919 The Third Aliyah begins, consisting mostly of Jews from Russia.

1920 The British Mandate over Israel is issued; the Haganah (Jewish defense organization) is founded.

1921 Arabs riot against Jews in Hebron, Jerusalem, and Jaffa.

1922 League of Nations grants Britain a mandate for Palestine.

1923 The Third Aliyah ends; the Palestine British Mandate officially comes into force; Britain divides Palestine into two districts, the eastern three-fourths of territory for Transjordan and the rest set aside for a Jewish national homeland.

1924 The Fourth Aliyah begins, consisting mostly of Jews from Poland.

1928 The Fourth Aliyah ends.

1929 Arabs riot in Jerusalem, Hebron, and Safed.

1932 The Fifth Aliyah begins, consisting mostly of Jews fleeing Nazi Germany and neighboring countries.

1936 Arab militants begin instigating anti-Jewish and anti-British riots, which go on for three years.

1937 The British Peel Commission recommends the partition of Palestine.

1939　The Fifth Aliyah ends; World War II begins; the Holocaust in Europe begins; a British White Paper limits Jewish immigration into Palestine and restricts Jewish land purchases.

1941　The Palmach (Jewish military force) is created.

1945　World War II and the Holocaust in Europe end; the League of Arab States is formed in Cairo, Egypt; the British limit Jewish immigration into Palestine to fifteen hundred persons a month.

1946　The British government resists increased Jewish immigration from Europe to Palestine; the Irgun (Jewish militant organization) bombs the King David Hotel in Jerusalem, which houses the British military command and the Mandatory government secretariat.

1947　Britain announces it will end its mandate for Palestine and refers the future of Palestine to the United Nations; the Irgun and Stern Gang fighters massacre more than a hundred Palestinian villagers in Deir Yassin near Jerusalem; the United Nations votes to partition Palestine into independent Jewish and Arab states; Arabs riot in Jerusalem and blockade the city; the war for independence begins.

1948　May 14: The British mandate ends; the State of Israel is proclaimed; hundreds of thousands of Palestinians flee; the United States and the Soviet Union recognize Israel.

May 15: Egypt, Jordan, Syria, Lebanon, and Iraq invade Israel.

1949　Israel's first national elections take place; the first 120-seat Knesset (parliament) goes into session; Chaim Weizmann is elected the first president of Israel; David

Ben-Gurion becomes the first prime minister of Israel; Israel signs armistice agreements with Egypt, Lebanon, Jordan, and Syria; the War of Independence ends; Israel takes its seat as the fifty-ninth member of the United Nations.

1950   Transjordan annexes the West Bank and renames it the Hashemite Kingdom of Jordan.

1952   The mass immigration to Israel from Europe and Arab countries ends.

FOR FURTHER READING

Books

J. Bowyer Bell, *Terror Out of Zion: The Fight for Israeli Independence*. Piscataway, NJ: Transaction, 1996.

Michael T. Benson, *Harry S. Truman and the Founding of Israel*. Westport, CT: Greenwood, 1997.

Alan Dershowitz, *The Case for Israel*. Hoboken, NJ: Wiley, 2003.

Martin Gilbert, *Israel: A History*. New York: Morrow, 1998.

Eunice Holliday, *Letters from Jerusalem During the Palestine Mandate*. London: Radcliffe Press, 1997.

Efraim Karsh and Rory Miller, eds., *Israel at Sixty: Rethinking the Birth of the Jewish State*. New York: Routledge, 2008.

Adam LeBor, *City of Oranges: An Intimate History of Arabs and Jews in Jaffa*. New York: Norton, 2007.

Aaron Levin, *Testament at the Creation of the State of Israel*. New York: Artisan, 1998.

Benny Morris, *Birth of the Palestinian Refugee Problem, 1947–1949*. Cambridge: Cambridge University Press, 1987.

Benny Morris, ed., *Making of Israel*. Ann Arbor: University of Michigan Press, 2007.

Sari Nusseibeh with Anthony David, *Once upon a Country: A Palestinian Life*. New York: Farrar, Straus, and Giroux, 2007.

Amos Oz, *A Tale of Love and Darkness*. New York: Harcourt, 2003.

Itamar Rabinovich, ed., *Israel in the Middle East: Documents and Readings on Society, Politics, and Foreign Relations, Pre-1948 to the Present*. Waltham, MA: Brandeis University Press, 2007.

Ahmad H. Sa'di and Lila Abu-Lughod, *Nakba: Palestine, 1948, and the Claims of Memory*. New York: Columbia University Press, 2007.

Edward W. Said, *After the Last Sky: Palestinian Lives*. New York: Columbia University Press, 1999.

Tom Segev, *1949: The First Israelis*. New York: Henry Holt, 1998.

Tom Segev, *One Palestine, Complete: Jews and Arabs Under the British Mandate*. New York: Henry Holt, 2000.

Avi Shlaim, *The Iron Wall: Israel and the Arab World*. New York: Norton, 2000.

Sandy Tolan, *The Lemon Tree: An Arab, a Jew, and the Heart of the Middle East*. New York: Bloomsbury, 2006.

Ben Wicks, *Dawn of the Promised Land: The Creation of Israel*. New York: Hyperion, 1997.

Periodicals

Haim Baram, "Israel's Secret Fears," *New Statesman*, May 19, 2008.

Richard Boudreaux and Ashraf Khalil, "For some Palestinians, One State with Israel Is Better than None," *Los Angeles Times*, May 8, 2008.

James Barker, "The Bombing of the King David Hotel," *History Today*, July 2006.

Ethan Bronner, "After 60 Years, Arabs in Israel Are Outsiders," *New York Times*, May 7, 2008.

Jeffrey Goldberg, "Prophesying Palestine," *Atlantic Monthly*, April 2008.

Ruth Gruber, "The Birth of a Nation, 1948," *New York Times*, May 18, 2008.

Muhammad Hallaj, "Recollections of the Nakba Through a Teenager's Eyes," *Journal of Palestine Studies*, Autumn 2008.

Ray Hanania, "All Palestinians Not Living in Palestine Are 'Refugees' of al-Nakba," *Washington Report on Middle East Affairs*, May/June 2008.

David Horowitz, "Founding the New State: An Expert's Estimate of the Tasks Ahead," *Commentary*, February 1948.

Efraim Karsh, "1948, Israel, and the Palestinians—the True Story," *Commentary*, May 2008.

Rashid Khalidi, "Palestine: Liberation Deferred," *Nation*, May 26, 2008.

Elias Khoury, "For Israelis, an Anniversary. For Palestinians, a Nakba," *New York Times*, May 18, 2008.

Tim McGirk, "The Long View," *Time*, May 19, 2008.

Walter Russell Mead, "Change They Can Believe In: To Make Israel Safe, Give Palestinians Their Due," *Foreign Affairs*, January/February 2009.

Benny Morris, "Why Israel Feels Threatened," *New York Times*, December 29, 2008.

Greg Myre, "Israel's Acting Leader Backs Creation of Palestinian State," *New York Times*, January 24, 2006.

History Today, "Foundation of the State of Israel," May 1998.

Ilene R. Prusher, "Two Loyalties Tug at Arabs Who Are Israeli, Too," *Christian Science Monitor*, May 6, 1998.

Romesh Ratnesar, "The Dawn of Israel," *Time*, March 31, 2003.

Kermit Roosevelt, "Will the Arabs Fight?" *Saturday Evening Post*, December 27, 1947.

Nancy Salvato, "A Brief History of the Israeli-Palestinian Conflict," *World & I*, May 2006.

Zohar Segev, "American Zionists' Place in Israel after Statehood: From Involved Partners to Outside Supporters," *American Jewish History*, September 2007.

David K. Shipler, "A Conflict's Bedrock Is Laid Bare," *New York Times*, May 27, 2001.

Ruth R. Wisse, "Forgetting Zion," *Commentary*, October 2008.

Web Sites

Behind the Wall (www.lifebehindthewall.org). On this site, Palestinian teenagers share their thoughts and feelings about a broad range of topics, including their religion, freedom, and the Arab-Israeli conflict.

Eye 2 Israel (www.israel1.org). On this site, Israeli teenagers share their experiences growing up in Israel and their thoughts on many different topics, including the Arab-Israeli conflict and coexistence.

Israel Ministry of Foreign Affairs (www.mfa.gov.il/MFA). This site features facts about Israel, information about its history and government, and much more, including historical documents.

MidEastWeb (www.mideastweb.org). This site contains news, history, analysis, dialogue, bibliography, maps, statistics, culture, and opinions about Israel and Palestine, as well as links to an e-zine, articles, and other sites for further information about the Middle East.

INDEX